Mother Angelica's Guide to the Spiritual Life

Also by Mother Angelica:

Praying with Mother Angelica
Meditations on the Rosary, the Way of the
Cross, and Other Prayers

Mother Angelica on Christ and Our Lady

Mother Angelica on Suffering and Burnout

Mother Angelica's Quick Guide to the Sacraments

Mother Angelica on Prayer and Living for the Kingdom

Mother Angelica on God, His Home, and His Angels

Mother Angelica's Practical Guide to Holiness

Mother Angelica's Answers, Not Promises

A Holy Hour with Mother Angelica

Living the Scriptures

Mother M. Angelica

Mother Angelica's
Guide to the Spiritual Life

Edited by Brandon McGinley

EWTN PUBLISHING, INC.
Irondale, Alabama

paperback ISBN 978-1-68278-230-9
ebook ISBN 978-1-68278-231-6
Library of Congress Control Number: 2021940985

First printing

Contents

1

Faith Is a Struggle

So often, when we read Scripture, we read it in a way that makes it unreal. It's all inspiration, except there are human beings in that book, sinners, like yourself: people who had to struggle against anger and resentment and difficulty in forgiving. They even had difficulties that some of you don't even have, and yet you see God using them to do great things for the Kingdom.

Did you ever see somebody who seemed unusually holy? I don't mean that they have a halo, but that you just know that when you are in their presence, you're somehow with God. And yet, they'll lose their patience once in a while, or they are a little irritable, or some other thing that you don't equate with holiness. You think the saints are always very pious, never flustered, never anxious, never worried about tomorrow. That's not realistic.

I see in the saints, and I see in all the Scriptures, men and women who are full of blood and guts and fears and anxieties. And you know, so many of them had the same kind of fears you have. They had fears of failure, and they went on. You know Gideon was like that. Gideon was a man who was just scared. Saul was scared. David was scared. So often throughout the Old Testament, the prophets, as they struggled to proclaim the message of the Lord, were scared!

Your fears and the fears of all the great people in the Old Testament and the New Testament are very similar. You're not alone in being human. You're not alone in being imperfect, in your struggles, in your temptations, in all those anxieties and tensions! You know that all the saints had tension, but they became holy with these things. So we need to change our attitude about what holiness is all about.

You can overcome all of these things—not by destroying them, not by never having them, but by learning how to make choices. You and I have been destined by God to make choices, the right choices, and all of these moments are opportunities for you to make a choice between the world, the flesh, and the devil on the one hand, and God. God is the One you choose. And when you choose God over all of these things, that is what we call holiness.

Today we live in a society that has taught us to be soft. There's no challenge anymore. There's no guts in anything. That's the eighth gift of the Holy Spirit—guts! There's no enthusiasm and no zeal! We're scared to death of failing. Ah, if all you can do is fail, you're ahead. I have never failed in a way that I haven't also learned a lot. Success I'm afraid of, but failure I'm not afraid of. I'd much rather begin something, even if I can't finish it. Someone asked me, "You know, Mother, what will you do if this television ministry you've begun flops?" And I said, "Well, I will have the most lit-up garage in the world." You see, we're obsessed over flopping. That's what holiness is to us today: to never fail! But that's like being an Egyptian mummy; it's not saintly.

I go to the lives of saints, and I look in between the lines to find the men and the women who struggle like I struggle. I'm Italian by descent. There's no patient Italian in the whole world. We're a hot-tempered, volatile, loud people. To us, eating is an art. You know, some people are so terribly scrupulous about eating. I don't mean you have to eat a whole pie, but you sure should praise God for that one slice you ate.

You see, to be holy means God is in everything. But today we're afraid; we don't want to be fanatics. Today you can't tell a Christian from a pagan. You really can't. Do you realize what the Lord said? Imagine Jesus today standing in the middle of Jerusalem. Remember all the hatred, war, and fear in that city, and all the surrounding areas. And suddenly the God-Man, Jesus, gets up in front of a crowd and says: "Happy are the poor in spirit, theirs is the Kingdom of Heaven. And blessed are the gentle; they shall inherit the land." Today we are taught to go out and get it! Lie, cheat, and steal, but get it! Blessed are the poor? Applesauce!

And Jesus continues, saying that you're happy when you mourn over your sins. What sins? You don't want to hurt people's feelings or make them feel guilty. Let them go to Hell, but don't make them feel guilty. Don't tell anybody that he's committing adultery; he's "in love." (Really? I would have never guessed it.) Don't tell a child not to take dope; you'll "inhibit" him. I had a woman come to me with the saddest sentence I ever heard. She wanted me to pray for her son, a beautiful man. She said to me, "I could handle him when he was on dope. But now I can't!" And I said, "What's he on?" She said, "Jesus." What a sad statement. I said, "You are sick! You're really sick!" Because to be a Catholic Christian, when you have the sacraments, is to be so full of joy that the whole world can go to pot, including the economy, and you are still praising God! Sure you suffer, but you are not afraid because Someone you are in love with is there with you.

But faith is still a struggle. You mustn't be afraid when you question faith, when you question what you're doing or what God is doing in your life because that's human, and it's normal. It's what you do after you question. You say to yourself, "I wonder why God is permitting this? I wonder why this has happened to me?" You feel anger coming up, because you're human and finite, and you can't understand wisdom. It's like living in the valley and then being guided by someone on top of the mountain who can see more than you do. But it's difficult when you are down there, as if you had blinders on.

But now, after that doubt arises in your heart, if you say, "Lord, I really don't understand, but I know You love me, and I know that You will bring good out of my mistakes, out of this situation, out of other people's mistakes." If, at that point, you can go on in peace, that is faith! That is real faith, because it is indicative of a soul who trusts God. And a soul who trusts God is invincible. Our Lord said that faith the size of a teeny mustard seed can move a mountain.

Faith is a struggle: just look at the apostles. I love St. Paul and St. Peter because they seem to me to be so human, so full of struggle, so full of those anxieties that you and I have. The Epistle to the Ephesians is glorious! Paul had caused a riot in Ephesus because he was destroying idols of the goddess Diana. Paul was a short man, so imagine a room with people yelling and shouting, "Let's get at this little man!" Paul had problems not only from the perils of the apostolate, not only from the perils of his own nation, who looked at him as a traitor, but even from the Christians. Some thought that he didn't really have a right to call himself an apostle. Now we look at Paul and say, "Oh, what a great man! What a theologian, what a mystic." But in those days, he was a half-pint who was causing riots and disturbances and was considered suspicious by all sides.

The man had frustrations that you and I can't even imagine. In Second Corinthians he asked the Lord three times to take his pain from him, but the Lord told Paul that His power is at its best in human weakness. How come you and I get so discouraged? How come you and I, after we read that, always think it applies to somebody else but never to us?

When you make the right choice when you're tempted to any kind of sin, that's holiness! And call a sin a sin, will you? Don't say, "That's my human nature." You have to call a spade a spade.

If you start kidding yourself, then you're never going to have that beautiful experience with God's grace and mercy. You're always going to wonder. You're always going to feel small, and want to feel big, and never quite make it. And your whole life will be a kind of battle between what you are inside and what people think you are, between what you think you are and what you want to be. What a waste of time! Wherever you are, no matter what a great family you live in, no matter how ideal your situation, your work, whatever, you've still got that inner struggle.

But if you're in love which Jesus, you can overcome the fear that's in faith; you can overcome the discouragement that wrapped around hope; and you can overcome the difficulty in love, because you are not alone. Jesus is with you. Do you think He came and redeemed us, and just opened some great big gate to the Kingdom and said, "Now, y'all come"? No! He did more than that! He came so that you and I could be temples of His Spirit.

Just imagine that. Can you imagine God, Who created the universe, in all its majesty, being inside you? That's the witness of a Christian. The witness of a Christian's faith is to live by the truth that God lives in you and to believe it to the point where you would never do anything to scandalize or to belittle the Spirit Who lives in you. That means that you must be aware of your dignity as a Christian. I wonder if it's because we're not aware of that that we are not really changing the world? If you're not transformed, you can't transform anyone else, because they don't see anything they want in you.

The people in the early Church were not converted by sermons. They were converted by the joy of the Christians, by their ability to suffer. Faith must have been difficult in those days, terribly difficult! Just imagine knowing that if you were caught being a Christian, you could be thrown to the lions. And yet they went on. They dug underground so that they could worship secretly. And when they were caught, they went joyfully to be chewed up by lions!

Oh, you and I would give up the Faith. We would say, "Oh, look! I was better off before I was a Christian." But see, that's part of the nitty-gritty aspect of faith. That's part of the challenge. We don't have a challenge anymore. I'm sure those first Christians were afraid. When they were in the arena with the crowds yelling and screaming for their blood, and the iron doors opened up, I think they were scared. I think they clung to one another to give each other support. And when those lions came down, I think they shook in their boots. But they were there.

Don't be afraid because you're afraid. Don't think you have little faith because you don't have the end in view. Don't think that you lack faith because you don't understand God's ways. That's not hard. If you understood His ways, you would be God.

If a small child doesn't know which way to go and all of a sudden sees his tall father, as soon as the child puts his hand in his father's hand, he feels safe. He feels secure. He has hope. He has the warmth of love. Nothing has changed: The child does not see anything more than he saw before. He still does not know where he's going. He still doesn't see the end. And yet there is in him a confidence, a trust that he didn't have before. And in his little heart, he knows he's still uncertain. He knows he still doesn't see the end. But because he's not alone, and he has his father's hand, and he feels the warmth of that love, he goes on taking one step at a time, in total faith, knowing it will be all right.

That's what faith is all about. The apostles had that kind of faith; Abraham had it; all the saints had it. It's the kind of faith that says, "My Father loves me, and though I do not know the end and I don't understand what's happening to me, I know He loves me. And He is not only standing beside me but standing within me."

2

God's Greatest Attribute

Mercy is a very difficult virtue for the average human being, but it's God's greatest attribute. (I think it is, anyway.) We'll begin with something from St. John's Gospel that is an example of God's beautiful mercy: the story of the woman caught in adultery.

Early in the day, Christ was in the Temple and crowds of people rushed down there to see Him, waiting for the great message. Suddenly, a mob dragged a woman in. "Teacher, this woman has been caught in the act of adultery" (John 8:4). Can you imagine that woman? You know, some of you people goof off a little bit, but nobody knows about it. But the very thought that somebody may see you coming out or going somewhere, or doing this or that, ah, it scares you to death. There's a fear that grips your heart. Well, this woman was caught in the very act of adultery. Can you imagine her pounding heart and her fear, knowing that she is about to be stoned, stoned to death?

(You know what gripes me? I wonder what happened to the man. I always wondered why they didn't stone him to death too. But anyway, I won't go into that.)

The Pharisee said to Jesus, "Now in the law Moses commanded us to stone such. What do you say about her?" (John 8:5). They are out to get Jesus, and they thought they had Him. They're going to do two things at once: kill this woman and get Jesus by forcing Him, the God of mercy, to contradict Moses.

Now, you have to understand something about this story. When Jesus looked at them and looked at her, He knew their hearts. He knew that some of those men had done the same thing and worse. And He just looked at them very calmly and began to write on the ground. (I always wondered what He wrote.) And they began to leave, one by one. And then only the woman is left, standing before Him. And He says, "Woman, where are they? Has no one condemned you?" And she said, "No one, Lord." He says, "Neither do I condemn you..." (John 0.10-11).

Now, too often we stop there with Jesus' words to the woman. A lot of you people are committing sins, maybe even adultery, and you think, "Ah, the Lord had mercy on this woman. I'll be fine." Don't you be presumptuous! This woman may have been totally ignorant of the law. She may have been used. But God knew this woman's plight. Don't presume that God is going to do the same with you. You got to put the period in the right place: The sentence continues, "Go, and do not sin again."

It's easy to read the Scriptures the way we *want* to read them. You must understand that God is merciful. His mercy is like the ocean, but you cannot presume on it! You can't just say, "I'm going to have a ball because God is merciful." No, because right in the middle of that ball, you might drop dead and not be able to say "I'm sorry." Now what are you going to do?

When I was a young novice, I'd get up at five in the morning, and it would be dark and cold, and I'd say, "Lord, today I'm going to be patient, come hell or high water." By nine o'clock came hell and high water. I blew it, every time. I said to the Lord, "How come, Lord, you have blessed me in beautiful ways, and yet I'm so impatient?" A sister would come up to me with a question she had on her mind, but I'd have some more important things to do and I would answer her, but always with an attitude, "What are you bugging me for now? Can't you see I'm busy?" And I'd always feel bad afterward, but you know you can't live your whole life afterward. You got to start doing something different now.

See, the thing with Christianity is that it is not enough that we change; we must become transformed. It is not enough just to know Jesus as Lord; Jesus must be Lord in my heart so that people see Jesus in me. If they don't see Jesus in me, where are they going to see Him? I want you to remember this one thing: You may be the only Jesus your neighbor will ever see.

And so, I went through that day asking myself, "What's wrong with me that I cannot be patient?" But I realized something. I realized I was generous. I was generous with things, with my talents, even with my thoughts; but I was not generous with my time. That's why I was so impatient. So then, when a sister would come to me and I felt like I was busy, or the phone rang and I wanted to rest, or someone came in with a problem and I wanted to pray, I realized that I had to be generous with time.

You see, all of us have some very big weaknesses that just bother our brothers something fierce. We don't always see them, but our brothers' weaknesses bring out our own. Isn't it wonderful that God gave you a thorn in your side somewhere? St. Philip Neri was a very angry man, and he went before the Blessed Sacrament and prayed for three hours for gentleness. "Lord, make me gentle." After three hours, he felt gentle, and he went out and met a very humble brother, and he blasted him about something he did that morning. And then he met a priest who didn't clean his chalice right, and he blasted him. Suddenly he realized, "I'm not gentle!" He ran back to the church and said, "Lord! I stayed here three hours praying for gentleness, and look what happened!" And the Lord appeared to Philip, and He looked at him and said, "Philip, you have prayed to me for gentleness, so I have multiplied the opportunities in which you can be gentle."

So, your neighbor or your husband or your wife is not a bore, a problem, or a nut. No, they are part of God's plan for pruning you.

They are opportunities. Now, I still feel impatient. (My impatience is going to die fifteen minutes after I do.) But God has not asked me not to feel; He has asked me to make *a decision*. And that decision is to love Him in the present moment. Every moment is like a new sheet of paper. Isn't that glorious? Don't worry about tomorrow. Don't live in the past. Don't worry about yesterday; it's all gone.

I love to go to the ocean. I remember being in California, and as I stood near the ocean, a drop of water hit my hand, and I looked at it. Then I looked at the ocean, and it was so big! And I looked again at this drop on my hand, and the Lord said to me, "Angelica, that drop for all your sins, all your imperfections, and all your frailties. Throw it into the ocean." I didn't want to keep that drop; it seemed like I shouldn't. So I threw it back. And then the Lord said to me, "Angelica, the ocean is my mercy; the drop was all your sins. Now, if you looked for the drop, would you ever find it?" And I said, "No, Lord." And He said, "If you looked and looked, would you not do yourself a disservice in me?" I said, "Yes, Lord." Then He said, "Why do you lament?"

You see, your sins and imperfections are like a drop in the ocean. Every day, every minute of the day, throw your drop in the ocean of His mercy. Don't worry! Just try harder. Give God the pleasure.

It says in St. Luke's Gospel, "Take heed to yourselves; if your brother sins, rebuke him, and if he repents, forgive him; and if he sins against you seven times in the day, and turns to you seven times, and says, 'I repent,' you must forgive him" (Luke 17:3–4). Then Peter chimes in. Peter was a man who wanted to make sure everyone knew he understood this lesson. Later, this time in Matthew's Gospel, he asked Jesus, "Lord, how often shall my brother sin against me, and I forgive him? As many as seven times?" (Matt. 18:21). He's just trying to be smart, now, showing that he remembers what Jesus said about seven times. But Christ responds, "I do not say to you seven times, but seventy times seven" (Matt. 18:22).

Wow! Can you imagine? I don't know if anyone has ever offended me that much.

Jesus then moved right into the parable of the unforgiving debtor (Matt. 18:23–35). It shows how there's something wrong with the way we usually think about mercy. Why is it that you and I have so much trouble forgiving? It's so hard for us to say, "I'm sorry." Is it pride? Are we kind of conniving? Are we trying to pretend? Are we saying, "God, now You've got to forgive me; but I don't need to forgive my brother because he treated me unjustly"? I think that we don't have the deep realization that we offend God.

Jesus said, "When [the king] began the reckoning, one was brought to him who owed him ten thousand talents." That would be millions of dollars today. "So the servant fell on his knees, imploring him, 'Lord, have patience with me, and I will pay you everything.'" Where is he going to get millions of dollars? But the king looked at him and forgave the debt. Can you imagine going to your banker and saying to him, "Look, don't take everything I've got! Don't take my home! I'll pay it all in time!" And the man looks at you and says, "Oh, you're never going to be able to pay such a huge debt. Forget it!" Oh, you just can't imagine!

Now, I wonder about the personality of this debtor in the parable, if he did not get in debt because he was a conniver, a cheat, and a liar; because a servant happened to meet him who owed him a day's wages — less than a hundred dollars or so. And he demanded, "Pay what you owe!" And the servant said, "Have patience with me, and I will pay you." Remember that this man was just forgiven millions! And he looks at this man who owes him a few bucks and took him to debtors' prison. Well, you're appalled at his lack of gratitude of course, and his lack of mercy! And you look at it and say, "Well, I can't imagine anyone doing that."

Now, look at that again. When you offend God, you're offending the Most High; you're offending the Creator of Heaven and earth,

Who has the power to annihilate you! And you say to Him, "I won't do what You ask, and I don't love You at this moment. I love myself." That's like those millions of dollars. And He says, "Look, I know there's no way you can pay me back. There's no way you can make reparation. I sent my Son, but you've got to be sorry." And so, you say you're sorry. You say, "Master, I offer You the Precious Blood of Your Son, Jesus. I have nothing to pay You with. Forgive me." And He says, "Okay, forget it. Just don't even remember it! And I'll tell you what, I won't remember it, either." Can you imagine that, all you sinners, myself included: the Lord is saying, "I won't even remember that you ever owed me a nickel—not a nickel!"

Now, here comes your wife, your child, your husband, your neighbor, your colleague, and they do some little bitty thing, like giving you a dirty look, just some little thing. And you look at them, and you're angry and unforgiving. Maybe you go to the supermarket and a bunch of prices have gone up. You go to the checkout and the clerk is a little irritable because everyone has been complaining, and now she's short-tempered. And then you're rude, and you don't forgive her. You go home and you're angry, and you don't go to that store anymore.

You see, we vacillate between unforgiveness and presumption. There are many who never say they're sorry, because they don't see God as demanding any forgiveness, any sorrow, any repentance. They think He's a great big man, with a great big beard, and He's looking down kind of dumbly, not conscious of what's going on. Wake up! Look, if you have been forgiven for your millions, you've got to forgive those few bucks. You just can't say, "Well now, I've just got one big, wonderful Father up there, and He has an ocean of mercy, and I can just go have myself a ball because God never sends anyone to Hell." Well, I hope you never find out you're wrong! Because by that time, down you are! There's no way up!

You see, we've got crazy ideas about the Scriptures because we never read them right! We never put our own lives into them, our own frustrations, our own lack of mercy. We read them like a newspaper and say, "Oh, that man was cruel." Oh, really? I hope you don't say that too loud, because the Lord's going to look at you and say, "You're right, and you've got the same problem!" Your kid comes home late. You are worried, and you should be worried. But then you holler at him, and he's angry with you, and there's a tremendous quarrel. Nobody forgives. He should forgive, and you should forgive. Why don't you say, "I'm sorry"? Why don't you say, "You're forgiven. Now let's begin again. Let's not bring the same stuff up"? Remember, God loves you.

3

Excuses, Excuses

You know, there ought to be a prize today for people who make excuses—because I think we'd all win something. We are in the habit today of making excuses. And because our faith is weak, we excuse ourselves from answering God's call, from doing God's will, from listening to the Church, from listening to the Gospel. We come up with all these fantastic reasons why we don't have to be good; why Christians don't have to be Christians; why we don't have to strive; why we don't have to go that extra mile that God is asking us to go—to show that extra bit of compassion or that extra bit of love, to do that extra bit of work. And so, we make excuses that are so comfortable that we can literally walk away and forget what God has asked us to do.

You know, the apostles were great men but very faulty men. That's why I love them! They remind me of myself, and I hope they remind you of yourself! Look at St. Paul in Second Corinthians, and you'll find a man who had an excuse not to be a real Christian. He talks about being shipwrecked and beaten, in danger of floods and robbers and storms. Oh, the man had all kinds of excuses not to be a Christian, not to continue, not to persevere.

Sometimes we can't make a distinction between the "reality" that means the actual obstacles that keep us from being good, from being a Christian, and from striving for sanctity, and the "reality" that is really the excuses that blur the truth. We put up a smoke screen and say, "Well, I don't need to listen to that, because it doesn't look *real.*" For example, a lot of people criticize us for depending upon God's providence, and they say, "But you see, you have to have visible means of support, and a visible this, and a visible that!" But you see, God is always visible in the present moment—visible in your eyes, visible in you, visible in His creation! How visible do you want God to be? God is visible! St. Paul says in Romans, "Ever since the creation of the world his invisible nature, namely, his eternal power and deity, has been clearly perceived in the things that have been made" (Rom. 1:20).

Sometimes in your life and mine, God calls us to do the ridiculous. And that's what makes us a witness to the world, because the world looks at us and says, "Hey! You can't do that!" Ah, but it's being done! You say to yourself, "I can't overcome this temptation. I can't overcome alcohol, or drugs, or something else." And the world says, "Yeah, you're right. You can't do it." But God can! God says, "You can with my power, and my grace, and my presence; you can do all things, if you let me bear fruit."

You know, Our Dear Lord asks us so often to do the ridiculous, and we're afraid! I don't like to see things done for God done like the General Motors Corporation. You know what the Lord said to the apostles? "Carry no purse, no bag, no sandals" (Luke 10:4). Just imagine, those disciples were ready to go out again in the crowds with Jesus and be in the "in group" again, as they had been. And the Lord looks at them and says, "Boys, we're going to do something different today. I'm going to send you out two by two. Go preach the Good News." That was it. There was nothing else. Imagine that! He didn't say where to go, or when, or what to say. He gave them no money. You can't do anything without money!

My favorite Scripture is the appearance of Jesus on the shore of the Sea of Tiberias after the Resurrection. Peter says in frustration,

"I am going fishing" (John 21:3). You can see how beautifully human Peter was. I love that man. He was hot tempered, loud, impulsive, and so holy that his shadow healed people! And here's Peter, after the Resurrection, done waiting for the next thing to happen. "I am going fishing." And John says, "We will go with you" (see John 21:3). Can't wait all day. If Christ is going to come, He'll come.

And they went out in the boat, and they caught nothing. (There is not one place in Scripture where those beautiful apostles ever caught any fish on their own!) "Just as day was breaking, Jesus stood on the beach; yet the disciples did not know that it was Jesus" (John 21:4). Imagine this! The apostles are in a boat, and they see a figure on the shore. They had been out all night and they caught nothing, and they were cold and shivering.

And the stranger said, "Children, have you any fish?" Can you imagine being in a boat all night, catching nothing, and then having somebody ask you that? I would have said, "It's none of your business!" I would have said, "I didn't go fishing! I went out to meditate." The world teaches you to fake it: Never admit that you're human; never admit that you struggle; never admit that you fail. But do you know what Peter did, that beautiful man? He just said, "No!"

So they have just admitted failure to a stranger. And then Jesus said, "Cast the net on the right side of the boat." This was the wrong side, in shallow water! There's not a minnow there! But they listened and dropped the net. Either they were absolutely the worst fishermen in God's world, or they were simple, loving, holy men, not afraid to fail. They threw it out in shallow water at the wrong time on the wrong side of the boat. "So they cast it, and now they were not able to haul it in, for the quantity of fish. That disciple whom Jesus loved said to Peter, 'It is the Lord!'" (John 21:6–7).

There are times in your life and mine when it seems like twenty times each day you have to tell the Lord, "Lord, I can't do it. I have failed. It is beyond me!" And then He tells you to do something else seemingly ridiculous. "Don't worry, trust me; trust more. I'll take care of your children, your future, your pain, your worries, your heartaches, your frustrations. Trust me just a little more. Throw your net on that starboard side, in that shallow water, at the wrong time of day. Don't be afraid!"

God is going to ask you during your life over and over, "Throw that net on your starboard side. Trust me with something that you're sure cannot happen, and it's not going to change." See, God works with failure. I know it; you know it. The people in the Old Testament knew it. But when we read the Old Testament, we never read the blood and guts; we never read the failure. We only read about the great successes. Abraham waited, and waited, and waited. Finally, finally, in his old age, he had a son. But we only read that he had a son. Next time you read, think about the frustration in the man's heart, with a nagging wife after him all the time.

Think about Noah. God tells him: Why don't you go and build a boat in your backyard? I mean a big boat, three stories high! And then people will pass by for the next hundred years and say, "What are you doing?" And you'll say, "I am building a boat." "What for?" "For the flood." "For the flood? What flood? We're basically in a desert!" You might think that since it was God who told Noah, it would be easy. No! God may tell you something, but it doesn't take away the frustration that follows after the fact, the frustration of actually doing it and looking foolish. I bet Noah's kids got on his nerves. "Daddy! What are you doing?" "I'm building a boat." "What kind of a boat?" "A boat for animals." "Animals?" Can you imagine a boat full of animals? No air conditioning, no deodorant, nothing to make it smell good. Then, even after the flood came, he had to be worried about how long he was going to be in that thing. When we read it, we already know it'll be forty days until the floods recede. But he didn't know that — and he was in there for a lot more than forty days, because the waters had to go down!

We need to be able to imagine the human element in doing God's will. When we read Scripture, we look only at the elevated aspect of any story. We look forward to the end, but we forget about the beginning, the guts part. When we take the guts—the humanity, the weakness, the struggle—out of Scripture, we take them out of our own spiritual lives. We feel like we don't deserve God's attention, like we aren't fit for holiness. But your human nature, as weak as it is, is part of sanctity!

Let's go back to St. Paul in Second Corinthians. Here is a man who loved these Corinthians, but they have been criticizing him. Now, what is criticism except a hurt in the heart? It means that somebody I love doesn't think too well of me, or that something I've said or done hasn't sat well with somebody I love. Here is Paul, and somebody had accused him of exploiting the Corinthians. He was a man who worked hard, and he was fiery, and hot-tempered, and angry, just as you and I can be. But he loved the Corinthians, and he saw that frustration as part of growth.

But he did not rest in his frustration. See, that's where you and I make our mistake. What we do is rest in it so that we become resentful. And when we're resentful, we come up with all kinds of excuses to answer for our lack of zeal, and we forget God's call to holiness. God is calling you and me to great heights of holiness, *with* our human nature. He does not intend for you to destroy it; He intends for you to conquer it! He intends for you to do the ridiculous so He can manifest His presence, His providence, His love, and His mercy in our lives.

You're supposed to be a witness to God! Not only has He called you, but *through* you, He calls your neighbor to great sanctity and great holiness—and sometimes to bug you. And it's our neighbors' weaknesses and falls that should bring forth the very best in us, not the worst in us. Don't let your neighbor be an excuse for you to indulge in your weaknesses, because God is calling you to great things in this world, great things in the Kingdom, great holiness of life. Greatness is what God has destined you for.

4

Cracked Pots

"But we have this treasure in earthen vessels, to show that the transcendent power belongs to God and not to us" (2 Cor. 4:7). Here's what St. Paul is trying to tell us: We're cracked pots that hold the treasure of God's divine life within us. (Don't go looking for "crackpot" in Scripture! I'm saying we're "cracked pots.") An earthen vessel is a thin little thing, fragile and imperfect. But that's St. Paul's point: He's trying to make us understand that we are imperfect.

You think, "Well, I'm imperfect so I can't be holy," or "God doesn't love me," or "He doesn't live in me." You have all these excuses tucked away in your heart and your mind. But the apostles struggled, and the saints struggled, and you struggle, and I struggle, and the whole world struggles to be holy. We're just not going to make it overnight. Rome wasn't built in a day, and neither will you be.

I want to talk about the woman at the well. Scripture says that "Jesus, wearied as he was with his journey, sat down beside the well" (John 4:6). (Can you imagine God tired? It's very hard to know that someone would love me so much He wanted to feel like I feel.) "There came a woman of Samaria to draw water" (John 4:7). Now, a Samaritan woman would have been a heretic. And Jesus looked at her and said, "Give me a drink." And she looks at Him and says, essentially, "What? Why? You're a Jew." In those days, a Jew would never ask a Samaritan for a drink. There was a tremendous amount of prejudice. And here Jesus broke down prejudice.

You know, you and I can be prejudiced in our own families. You can write off your children as hopeless, or you can write off your husband as an old goat. (But see, you look at yourself in the mirror tomorrow morning, and you don't look so hot yourself.) The most beautiful thing a family can do is to be what God made them to be, including growing old together! Nobody wants to be old today. But part of family life is living and being old (or young) and being not just accepted but loved as you are. See, we're trying to make the young grow fast, and we're saying to the old, "You've had it." We have to be family first in our heart, but that starts with being family with Jesus, family with the Trinity.

The Trinity lives in you and me! If only we were alive to the truth that the Father, the Son, and the Spirit live in us just as in a church! When we go into church, we genuflect because we know there is a presence. And that presence is Jesus in the Sacrament, but that presence is also in your neighbor. Do you realize what it would be like if you put the holy and the human together? It would be you! Our concept of saints is all-holy, all-divine; and our concept of ourselves and our families is all-human. So we cannot conceive of the saints as being faulty.

There's the story of Zebedee, who's mending his nets with his two sons, who are all ready to take over the business so he can retire (Matt. 4:21–22). Here comes a rabbi who looks at his two sons and tells them to follow Him. And Zebedee looks up and sees James and John just going off with the stranger. He can't believe it! And he gets angry and says, "Where are you going, you idiots?" (Now, don't look for that in Scripture.) But Jesus did call the brothers "sons of thunder" (Mark 3:17).

You can't read the Scriptures without finding this human nature creeping, almost oozing, out of their pores. Oh, Our Lord must have been aggravated sometime. He was the Master, the Son of God, incarnate in human form to explain the mysteries of the Father to these people. Here is a vast crowd, thousands of people, and here is the in group, the apostles, sitting near the Lord. And everyone's saying, "Wow, it must be wonderful to be so close to the Master, to know so much!" But the Scripture says that, at night, when everybody had gone home and had digested what the Lord had said, the apostles would go to Him when He was tired and say, "Master, will You explain the parable to us again?" And I can imagine Our Dear Lord looking at them and saying, "I don't believe this."

You've got to read between the lines and see that Our Lord had to be absolutely and totally frustrated. Sometimes it comes through more clearly, such as when He asked the apostles, "Then are you also without understanding?" (Mark 7:18). He was tired; He was ready to go to bed; He was ready to just lay His head down and forget the crowds, and they come up asking for more explanations!

I'm not saying that you have to be frustrated, or that it's not wrong to be frustrated. I'm saying that it's part of our nature, that we can control it, but that there are many times when we have to understand that frustration will come no matter what—over your job, over your family, over your friendships, over your talents and weaknesses, over the traffic. Jesus came to give us Himself so that we would have the power of God in our hearts, but the difficulties are still there.

But what we end up doing is thinking that because we experience difficulty, holiness must not be for us. But faith is to have one foot on the ground, one foot in the air. It's more than an intellectual assent to truth: It's to believe what Jesus says and apply it to our lives. But there's always that scary feeling of uncertainty. People ask me, "Well, Mother, how do you know all this stuff you're doing is God's will?" I say, "Ask me next year, and then we'll know whether it was God's will." The Lord probably isn't going to come down and say; "Look now, sweetie, I want you to do this little thing for me." He gave you a brain, a memory, an intellect, a will. He gave you grace, His presence in you.

Do you realize that if you're a baptized Christian, you have sanctifying grace in you; part of God is in you! And it's a part that must shine. You can't be in love and not show it.

You know, now in Church we shake hands. What happens if you're next to someone you don't like? Or you just had an argument with your wife or your husband or your kids, and here comes that awful moment. "I've got to turn around and hug this guy?" You have a struggle inside that's really unnecessary because we think that holiness is never to feel angry, never to feel impatient, never to feel anything at all. But holiness is about recognizing those feelings and pressing forward in love anyway.

Not feeling anything: That's like a mummy. They're the same century after century. You can't be that way. You're alive. You're a person whom God created to be special. So special are you that He had you in His mind before time began; so special are you that He lives inside you; so special are you that He wants you to be like a big beam on top of a mountain for all men to see by.

Holiness is to struggle day after day, to forgive seventy times seven times; to be hurt and to say, "Lord, forgive my enemy; forgive the person who hurt me"; to be able to see yourself and not fall apart. All of that is holiness.

There are just so many saints and holy people in the past and the present. I think there are a lot of really holy people out there. You can't go downtown anywhere and not rub elbows with somebody who's holy — some earthen vessel, cracked and struggling, trying to keep the whole thing together but doing so confidently because they know Jesus. Jesus lives in them. And that's the Good News: that as we struggle and God pours grace into us and we rise and fall, God in His infinite mercy loves us, keeps us going, gives us strength and courage and joy. Be joyful! It won't hurt you! Even if you have a problem, smile at your neighbor!

Remember: You may be the only Jesus your neighbor will ever see. I'm going to say that many times, because I want you to know your dignity. I want you to know how great you are before God when He lives in you.

5

Correction with Love

Receiving correction hurts us right in the heart, but it's the secret of holiness. I don't mean you need to go around griping at people and letting everybody gripe at you. What I'm saying is that God Himself allows us to be corrected. What do you expect love to do? Love corrects! When your parents do not correct you, that's when you should worry. People—kids or other family members or friends—need to know that you love them enough to say, "Hey look, this is bad. You're going to hurt yourself," without taking away love. That's the point: When I correct somebody because I'm angry, I do not correct with love. I'm just getting something out of my system. But if I correct out of love, I can say it in the strongest way, and they know the difference.

Your family is never going to be perfect, but it can be happy and holy. So parents have to correct, but sometimes children also see things in you that are not just right. Don't feel bad because they may tell you about those things: They love you, too. I had a young postulant come to me one time, and she sat down and I said, "Can I help you?" She looked at me and she said, "Don't you feel well today?" I said, "Well, now that you mentioned it, not too well." I said, "Why?" "Well, you're so irritable," she said, "I just thought you might have a lot of pain." And I looked at her and I said, "Well thank you, honey. I'm sorry I was irritable. I didn't realize it. But

I don't think my pain is great enough to account for that." And I thought, "That child, even a postulant, loved me enough to tell me that something wasn't right today."

Again, I'm not saying you should go around and correct each other willy-nilly. Criticism, for example, is not correction. Criticism destroys. The media is all geared toward criticism. I want you to think of your neighbor, your children, your husband and try to cross off in your head all those things that you find wrong about them. I want you to look at your spouse and begin to see the very beautiful things that you have lost sight of. Only from that perspective of love and adoration can we correct well.

You see, husbands and wives can get so accustomed to each other that they become like wallpaper or old chairs—just around, there when you come home, useful for this or that. You get in these little ruts and take each other for granted, so when something goes wrong, you don't have the ability to see it and correct it with love.

We also tend to threaten or to punish people as a form of correction, and we really can't do that. The best form of correction is love. Yes, punishing a child for disobedience must sometimes be part of correction, but we must not do so out of anger. Children should know that we want them to be good out of love for the good (because we love them), not out of fear.

You know, I am Italian by temperament. And believe me, no Italian, at least not anyone I know, gets up in the morning feeling, "It's a wonderful day!" So, I wake up with a temper, and I wake up impatient. Either the alarm went off too soon, or it didn't go off at all, and I don't have time and there's just a thousand little things to annoy me. But do you know what corrects me? When one of my sweet sisters comes in and says, "Good morning, Mother," and she's smiling and looking at me with love. You know, something happens to me. Nobody has said anything to me like, "Why are you so impatient over your dumb shoes?" In fact, they probably didn't even notice yet that I was impatient. But love is a kind of force, and it has the power to heal.

Think about the sun. You go outside, lie on the beach, and even on a cloudy day those rays hit you and make you so brown it hurts. That's the way love is (except it doesn't make you hurt). Sometimes it works unseen and unnoticed, but it has tremendous healing properties. If you're having trouble in your families, sometimes what you need to do is just sit down and look at each other and say something very simple: "I love you." And do something for each other that says, "I really want you here!"

A man came to me who was having some little problems with his wife and his family. And I said to him, "Why don't you just go home early one night and bring them some candy or bring your wife some flowers, just anything." And he looked at me and he says, "Ah, they don't want me home." I said, "Oh, go on." So he goes and gets her a great big box of chocolates, and he comes in the house all enthused, and he walks into the living room, where everyone says, "Shhhh!" They're watching a television program and didn't want to be disturbed. That's a little thing—and they probably didn't mean anything by it—but it said to him, "I don't love you, and I don't want you in this room. I have more important things to do." See, there is a basic selfishness that is creeping up in our families that is so serious, and it's little, little things like going, "Shhhh."

Maybe your wife gets up in the morning one day and she looks a little bit haggard—and you don't look so hot yourself. You come down the steps feeling great, but she doesn't feel so hot. And she looks at you and says peevishly, "What do you want for breakfast?" And so now you're peevish. But you can't expect her to be always bubbly. What is loving correction in that moment? It's simply to sit down and say, "Well, I'd like an egg." (Maybe you want it on her head, but that's okay, as long as you don't say that!) Now she's going to notice that you were kind when she was ornery.

See, correction isn't just a matter of mouthing off. Anybody can correct that way. And when you correct that way, you get a lot of your inner anger out, but you don't always accomplish anything. Do you ever think, "I'm hollering at my kids all the time and nothing ever changes"? They don't pay any attention to you because they've shut you off. They know that even though the correction is justified, there is a personal anger mixed in, so they are not interested. That means, in that moment, they have not felt loved. And as a result, we go running around in a vicious circle. Our families never change; they're always full of fussing and fuming. Most people in families talk at each other on the way in or on the way out. They lack that community of sharing.

I remember talking to a couple who were going through a rough patch. They sat down in my office as far away from each other as possible on the sofa, glaring at each other. Finally, I said to the woman, "Why did you marry him? What was it about him that you liked?" She was shocked and didn't know what to say. See, she had filled her mind so much with everything that was wrong with him that all the good things had been blocked out. Finally, she looked at him and said, "He was very kind." And he looked as if a big light went on. And I said to him, "Why did you marry her?" And he thought a minute, a long minute. It was the same thing: Everything in the front of his mind was bad. But finally he said, "She's kind of homey. You know, she's motherly, and I loved her because she was just always there, always faithful." And I said to them, "Well, I want you to see again what you began to see long ago." Each one of us must go back, way back sometimes, to remember the good and to be able to say, "I love you just as I did before."

6

Looking in the Mirror

If you look at the people who became holy through the power of grace, these were always people who were not afraid to look at themselves. They combine self-knowledge with confidence in their dignity. You know, today we look for a dignity without weaknesses, without frailties. We think that dignity can come only with perfection, and we think we have to fit ourselves into some mold of what perfection looks like. But we never fit into someone else's mold, or to a mold that we set up in our minds.

Look at people like the Samaritan woman, who had a hard time facing herself. Today, we don't want to face ourselves. We don't want to say, "I am not perfect. I have faults." No, instead we have only positive thinking: "I'm going to be better tomorrow, and I'm going to be even better the next day." But you find yourself the same person day after day unless you combine the quest for your dignity with friendship with Jesus.

It's only when you have Jesus in your heart that you can see and find your real self—because only then are you not afraid to look at yourself. You're not going around pretending you're something you're not. With Jesus, though, we can have the guts to say, "I am an angry person, but with the grace of God and the power of His Spirit, I can become like Jesus!" You see, it's very important when you go around trying to find out who you really are that you have

Jesus in your heart. And when His hand and your hand are close together, you will find Him in you. You will always find your weaknesses, and you will have the courage to face them and not hedge.

When the Samaritan woman finds Jesus at the well, Our Lord talks about giving her living water. The Samaritan woman makes excuses: "Sir, you have nothing to draw with, and the well is deep. Where do you get that living water? Are you greater than our father Jacob?" And Jesus replies, "Whoever drinks of the water that I shall give him will never thirst" (John 4:11–12, 14). That's what holiness is in your family, living water, but you have to work at it! It's not just going to come out of nowhere! Happiness and joy are something you work for. Today we don't want to work. We're entertained to death. (That's why people watch too much television; that's why I want to be on it.)

One day I said to my sisters, "Let's go around and pick out three beautiful things in each other." I was amazed to see how beautifully they thought of each other. When it came to me, they said, "Mother, you're understanding, you're loving, and you're generous." And I said, "You're right!" But this is because I find them easy! God gave me these gifts. I began to wonder during the day, though, why I am so impatient? I began to realize that the reason I was impatient was because I was generous with my things and I was generous with my talents—but I was not generous with my time. And I realized that the very thing that God gave me that was good, I had squandered in one important area.

Think of three good things about yourself, and see if you're using them well or squandering them—or even using them against yourself. Usually, a husband and a wife each have something the other does not have. If you're calm, I'll bet you married a vivacious individual: That's what attracted you to her, but right now you wish she would stand still just once! Or you married this man because he was serene and calm, but after five years, you want to put a lit match under him. So, the very thing that made you love him, you can use against yourself and make yourself miserable. If you're vivacious and your husband is calm, what you need is a little bit of his calm, and he needs a little bit of your pep. But if you drew from each other, instead of going against each other, you would find a holy family.

Jesus was trying to get the Samaritan woman to admit her flaws—remember, she had had five husbands and was living with another man. She says, "Sir, give me this water, that I may not thirst, nor come here to draw" (John 4:15). Let's not talk about spiritual things, she's telling Him; let's just talk about things that don't really get to me. That's what's wrong with the world today: Let's talk around everything. Let's not get to the nitty-gritty, gutsy part of it. Do you know what Christianity is? It's blood and guts. Christianity is a challenge, and too often today we don't think of it as a challenge.

Christianity is Someone you're in love with: Jesus the Lord. And when you're in love with Jesus, you're going to love your spouse and your children more, because only the love of Jesus can make you love. And if we will not face truth in our lives, as this woman refused to face truth—she kept changing the subject—then we will never become that perfect image God chose you and me to be: so much like Jesus that when a neighbor looks at you, he sees God. That's your dignity! Don't let anyone rob you of your dignity as a son and daughter of God—no one.

I want to repeat that: No one should rob you of that dignity. And you can rob yourself of that dignity by becoming so self-centered that when you look for yourself, you try to find your dignity without Jesus, without your family, without your neighbor. You'll never find your true self that way. You can't isolate yourself and say, "I want to find myself, and it doesn't matter what anybody else thinks, says, or does." All you'll find is a grotesque monster—a monster that you are creating as you go along.

God made you to His Image, and He redeemed you so that the Spirit in you could give that image of Jesus to your neighbor. But instead, you and I run just like the Samaritan woman, always changing the subject, always blaming other people. See, you and I sometimes have problems with people because of ourselves. We feel, for instance, that our families or our colleagues bring out the worst in us. No, that person is bringing out the real you, and you don't like it, and that's a weakness! But see, it is that very weakness that can be a precious tool for growing in self-knowledge. You cannot know yourself unless there's some beautiful person out there who bugs you to death and makes you rise to a higher level, makes you make hard choices and brings you out of yourself so you can see yourself as you really are.

And that's good! How are you going to be like Jesus if you don't know what's wrong with you, if you're always going to run away, if you always want to be alone? You can't love when you're all by yourself: Whom are you loving? Love is something that has to be shared, and as soon as love is not shared, it begins to decrease. Further, love that is shared increases our self-knowledge. The problem with self-knowledge, of course, is that it hurts. I have never arrived at self-knowledge that didn't hurt. I just don't want to think that I'm not the best person in the whole wide world. I don't want to think that I am an impatient, angry individual. I want to think I'm a gentle person and that all my anger is totally justified. But I have to look at myself and say, "Hey, this is me." See, I have to have my virtues and my weaknesses work together—but I have to know them, first.

And I also have to have my family in mind. I have to be able to sacrifice and to give. You see, when you change, your family changes, and your neighbor changes. You bring with you to the Kingdom neighbors, family, and friends. You don't go by yourself. That's the power of a Christian. That's the power of your dignity as a child of God. When you're repentant, your neighbor sees humility and faith. When you're gentle, your neighbor sees an angry individual sacrificing by holding it in. Today they tell you to let it all out, to go where your feelings take you. But there's no control in that. We need discipline! It's not about the hard discipline that's only a list of don'ts. No, we need the Gospels and the discipline that comes from them, and from the Church, and from the Commandments. You and I have to have the courage to look at ourselves in the mirror of our souls.

Sometimes we can't even look at ourselves in the mirror on the wall. We can't stand the wrinkles; we can't stand the gray hair. You know, you can put all the dye in your hair and get all the face-lifts you want, but the same old body is looking in the mirror. Now, when God lets you see yourself, you must be able to look at that image without panic and without guilt, because you need to say, "Jesus, this is me, and I want to be like You. I want to be a source of power in my family. I want to be gentle. I want to be kind."

You know, you can also have too much of a virtue. You can be too generous. If a man gives his entire paycheck, which was going to be used for rent and gas and food, to a homeless person, that is too generous. And you say, "Oh, God's going to reward him!" But the gas and electric company aren't going to think that way. He has his family to think about, and he has his rent to pay: These are just debts and just obligations. Now, he could have given part of his pay, but to give all of it is to use a virtue to an excess.

You can do that with any good thing. Take compassion: Failing to correct someone, especially a child, because you don't want to hurt his feelings—that isn't compassion at all. It's a focus on human respect. You think more of people's opinions than you do of people.

Self-knowledge, whether it's the knowledge of a virtue or a weakness, can hurt you if you aren't confident in God's grace and don't use it as a tool to grow in holiness. Scripture says we are "earthen vessels" who hold a treasure (2 Cor. 4:7). Would you put a treasure in an earthen vessel? I wouldn't. If I had something that was very rare and I wanted to preserve it, I wouldn't put it in a fragile container. I'd box it up and put steel around it. But God didn't do that. He put the treasure of His presence in this earthenware jar—each of us. Isn't that consoling? Full of cracks, but still holding a treasure—and sometimes that treasure's obnoxious.

Jesus isn't obnoxious, but you can be, and you're part of the treasure too. Your human nature, made to the image and likeness of God, is a treasure. So you need to make choices. You need to ask God to touch your mind and touch your heart and touch your soul so that you can look at yourself without guilt and can look at Jesus with hope and love and deep faith that says, "Jesus, here I am. I have many good qualities and some not so good. Help those that are good to grow; help those that are not good to be transformed." In this way, you and I, as we go along in our lives, can give courage to others.

I know it's difficult to overcome weaknesses. But Jesus in you can do it because you are still a treasure in the eyes of God. He made you; He loves you; He died for you. Ask Him to give you the realization of the beautiful idea of your dignity as a child of God and how the human and the divine work together to transform not only you, but the entire world. For the whole world will be better or worse because of you.

Don't be afraid of those shadows in the dark; every one of us has a shadow and a fear somewhere. But as you and I go through that journey of life, let's ask Jesus every day to touch our minds and our hearts so that we can face ourselves, good and bad, with the joy of the Lord.

7

God Can Do It

Do you ever feel like you want something really bad, but you aren't really sure God can give it to you? There's a joke about a woman who had a big mountain behind her house, and she couldn't see the valley on the other side. She got angry, and she knew her Gospel so she said, "I'm going to pray, because the Lord said, 'If you have faith of a mustard seed, you can move a mountain'" (see Matt. 17:20). Well, she prayed, and the next morning she got up and there was that mountain sitting there, as big as ever. And she said, "That's what I thought. Ha, ha." You see, she didn't have any *actual* faith or trust in God.

Now let's talk about Zechariah, the great father of John the Baptist. I want to see if you don't think this way with your own life and your family. Families become hopeless today because people start to despair and say, "Well, there's nothing I can do!" Yes, there is. You can be holy! You may be the only one striving, but you're there. That only means you're like Jesus, and you cannot tell me that being like Jesus will not transform your neighborhood, your school, your parish, and your family.

Now, Zechariah had been married a long time but had no children. Imagine, husbands, that you wanted a son to carry on your name, and you and your wife prayed day after day after day. But nothing ever happened. Well, Zechariah went to offer incense in the Temple, as always. But this time, all of a sudden, an angel appears. How many of you have seen an angel? Here is a man who has had a longing in his heart for years and years and years. Suddenly, he sees an angel standing in front of him.

And the angel said, "Zechariah, do not be afraid." Imagine the old man there, his knees shaking, scared to death. The angel continued, "Your prayer has been heard" (Luke 1:13). Wouldn't that do something to you? But the angel's not finished; "And your wife Elizabeth will bear you a son, and you shall call his name John. And you will have joy and gladness, and many will rejoice at his birth; for he will be great before the Lord" (Luke 1:13–15). Can you imagine somebody telling you that about a son you were about to have? "And he will go before him ... to turn the hearts of the fathers to the children" (Luke 1:17).

You see, back then, they had the same problems you and I have today. Family life is disrupted because we're so busy being our own person. I never in my life saw so many people running around "looking for themselves." They are like dogs running after their own tails. I don't know if you know who you are, but I know who I am. I learned that in the first grade! I'm a child of God and an heir to the Kingdom. (You say, "That's just the *Baltimore Catechism*." Try it; it wouldn't hurt you a bit!) You have been chosen by God. You're somebody, yes, but you're also family. "No man is an island." You can't live alone. You don't live alone.

Sure, you love yourself, but it's only a love built in Jesus. And that love has to go out; you can't keep it to yourself. I never heard of keeping love to yourself. Even on a natural level, two people in love can't hide it. They can walk in a room without saying a word, and you know it. That's how it is with Jesus. See, a family is to be in love first with Jesus and then with each other. But if you don't have a tremendous volume of love coming from God, you don't have anything to give.

So Zechariah is being told that John the Baptist was going to bring all this together. Oh, wouldn't you just melt and say, "Blessed be God!"? Do you know what Zechariah said? "How can I be sure of this?" Can you imagine this angel here in all his beauty, telling this man all these wonderful things, and he says, "How can I be sure?" My friends, this is a holy man I'm talking about, but even he didn't respond right. And haven't you done that to God? Hasn't He given you assurances sometimes, saying to you over and over in your heart, "Look, I know you're having a hard time. Things can't change right now, but I'll take care of it. Trust Me. Trust your children to me. Trust your future. Trust your past."

Not only does Zechariah ask for proof: He says, "I am an old man." (That must have been news to the angel, standing there looking at him with a long beard and all crumpled up.) He's not through yet. He says, "and my wife is advanced in years" (Luke 1:18). He's telling the angel: "Forget it, brother. I know you mean well, but this is impossible. See you the next time I'm in here." That's an imperfect man, but also, Scripture's saying, a holy man. You see, to struggle is a part of holiness.

Let me tell you, though, don't mess around with an angel, because here's how he responds:

I am Gabriel, who stand in the presence of God; and I was sent to speak to you, and to bring you this good news. And behold, you will be silent and unable to speak until the day that these things come to pass, because you did not believe my words, which will be fulfilled in their time. (Luke 1:19–20)

You know, we're an odd bunch of people. We pray for things, but we're so sure the Lord isn't going to do them that we even tell Him He can't do it. But we keep praying anyway. We all do that.

And see, God so often is prevented from doing the miraculous because you and I will not do the ridiculous.

Zechariah was an old man, and his wife was an old woman. That's what he tried to explain to the angel. But God can change the whole world just for you! I'm not saying He's going to do it, but He could! You see, sometimes a situation in your life feels so impossible that you obsess over it and forget about everything else. It's like a horse with blinders on. But if you say, "Lord, I am giving You an impossible situation. I know, though, that I must endure this situation—be it ever so painful, ever so difficult, ever so humiliating, ever so frustrating—as long as You need me to." Maybe it still seems like nothing happens—but something is happening. It's happening to you!

God is working on you all the time. I have frustrating moments every day. My desk is piled high with all kinds of papers, and one of my sweet sisters comes and cleans it up—but then I can't find a thing! All of my nice scraps get tucked away neatly, and it aggravates me to death! But I know God is telling me something—not only that I am not organized. He's also telling me, "Angelica, give your neighbor the opportunity of looking at your desk and not going, 'Ahhhh!'" That's a little thing. Then there are some situations in my life where I say, "Lord, if You can pull this off, believe me You're really something!" But you see, the very fact I have said, "If You can pull this off" is a kind of hesitation.

The important thing is this: we must never question what God can do, but we must wait in faith to see if He will. What's the difference? You question God's power when you say, "If you can." So many times we do what Zechariah did. But he even went further than that. He said, "I just don't think it can be done."

God may not answer our prayers the way we want. He may not answer on your time because sometimes He has to influence other people's wills; people are stubborn! God isn't just all of a sudden going to make a special magic formula and change their wills. God works very gently, and that takes time. So that means you've got to wait. In the meantime, you're saying to God, "I bet You can't do this," or "You won't do this." Well, He can do anything, but sometimes He also doesn't do it because it's not for your good.

I know sometimes the Lord has made me wait and wait and wait—and I know that during the waiting I learned a lot. I learned, first of all, that I was impatient, and hopefully I got a little more patience. I trusted God more, and myself less. When you pray, know God can do it! And if you look around with the eyes of faith, you can see how He's looking everywhere and doing everything for you, always for your good and mine.

8

God Chose You

Let's talk about being chosen. You see, God chose you to be; that's number one. He might have created billions of other people, but He made you. And of all the people living today, how many know Jesus? You know Jesus! Do you realize how many millions and millions of people do not know Jesus, do not have the benefit of the grace of God in their souls, do not know the saving power of Jesus, do not know the love of Jesus in the Father? You're especially chosen!

Now you've got to ask yourself why are you especially chosen. Well, the Scriptures tell us that you're chosen because God loves you. You're chosen because He wants to redeem you. God chose you because He has something great for you to do, something very great. In fact, in Colossians it says that we are "God's chosen ones" (3:12). Imagine yourself standing in a large group of people, and there on the stage is the king. And He's looking and looking, and all of a sudden, His eyes rest on you and your heart begins to leap. And he says, "You, come here." Ah, you'd be ecstatic. But that's nothing compared with what St. Paul is saying.

> Put on then, as God's chosen ones, holy and beloved, compassion, kindness, lowliness, meekness, and patience, forbearing one another and, if one has a complaint against

another, forgiving each other; as the Lord has forgiven you, so you also must forgive. (Col. 3:12–13)

What do you see when you see anyone? You see their clothing. You may like it or not like it, but you see what is on the exterior. What is a Christian clothed with? Well, it's your virtues, your compassion, your mercy, your gentleness, your forgiveness. And so Paul is saying, "These are clothing, and you should wear the garment of kindness and humility and so on." Oh, that's a hard virtue, humility! But it's the only way to get to the Father's heart: to be able to admit who you are, to know your weaknesses and your faults and still remember that God loves you. That's where we fall short. We are so conscious of our weaknesses that we think that God does not love us. That isn't true.

See, you're bought at a great price. We're told that in Scripture over and over and over. Jesus died for you! And, because He bought you at a great price, you have to understand that you're never alone. You are very, very special to God. But some of you who don't understand that think that God doesn't care. I get that feeling myself sometimes. I've said to Our Lord, "Look, don't You care? Whose side are You on?" I have myself been disheartened. But, in spite of the difficulties within and without, I try to keep my eyes on Jesus and know that Our Lord and Savior loves me, knows me, and has chosen me to be great in His eyes — to be holy, to be saintly, to be compassionate, and to be good.

See, faith is more than "an intellectual assent to truth." It's something alive! We don't have a goal; we don't have a vision. And Jesus is asking you to have a vision. I don't mean you need to have a vision of some saint or angel. No, I mean that you need a vision of what the world should be and of how you want to build your family, your soul, and the whole Church.

And you say, "Oh, I can't do that." You say, "Oh, God can't use me. Who am I?" You're a nobody, that's who you are, a miserable sinner, full of weaknesses, full of sins, full of frailties and infidelities. But still, God is looking for you. He is! His power is not great in somebody else's strength. His power is great in weakness (see 2 Cor. 12:9). So, we all measure up. And we need to say, "Lord, in all the realms of Thy creation, no one needs Thee more than I."

And, you know, the apostles were awfully weak men. Take the storm on the Sea of Galilee. It's a beautiful scene.

> On that day, when evening had come, he said to them, "Let us go across to the other side." And leaving the crowd, they took him with them, just as he was, in the boat.... And a great storm of wind arose, and the waves beat into the boat, so that the boat was already filling. (Mark 4:35–37)

I can imagine Peter, Andrew, and John—they're in this boat and they're rather calm. After all, Jesus is with them. I mean, what's to be excited about? Then come the waves. Peter looks at John, John looks at Peter, and they look at Jesus, snoring. Nobody says a word. Another wave comes, and Peter says to John, "Wake the Master." And John says, "What for? Nothing He can do." Peter says, "Well, get a bucket. We're going to drown together if we don't get this water out of this boat." And Jesus is still snoring. He's so tired.

Well, the apostles are not worried about Jesus. They're worried about themselves! I can just see them getting their buckets and getting that water out and looking at Jesus, and Peter is getting frustrated about not waking Him up. But John is strong and says, "No, don't wake Him up!" But another big wave comes, and they're almost knocked over and Peter yells, "Wake Him up!" And John says, "No!" In the meantime, Andrew is just trying to survive the storm outside the boat and the storm inside the boat.

Finally, Peter has had it. Here's a man who is not only tense but scared to death! He has had it with John, with Andrew, with the storm, and with Jesus! The Gospel says: "They woke him and said to him, 'Teacher, do you not care if we perish?'" (Mark 4:38). Can you imagine talking to God like that?

And Jesus woke up. I don't think He woke up in a hurry, though. You know, have you noticed in your life that sometimes the dear Lord pushes you almost to the brink, almost to that point where there's no other solution and nothing else to do? You're beset with problems and tribulations and you think, "Does He hear me? Does He care?" You and I have gotten to the position that Peter was in. "Master, don't You care?" is a question that is in everyone's mind sometime.

"And he awoke and rebuked the wind, and said to the sea, 'Peace! Be still!' And the wind ceased, and there was a great calm" (Mark 4:39). Can you imagine that? But the most fantastic sentence in this whole little story was still to come. Jesus says, "Why are you afraid? Have you no faith?" (Mark 4:40). Now, He didn't say "little faith." In many passages in Scripture He says "men of little faith," meaning they've got a little bit. But here He says "no faith." Now, I would think that if you were in a boat and the captain of the boat was asleep and the waves kept coming in and you were almost drowning, you'd have reason to be scared! Your life is a gift from God, and you should want to preserve it. But to question whether He cares, that is a different matter.

They did not believe that even though He seems to sleep, He watches and He cares. In your life and in my life, we think that because we're just as scared as the apostles were and because we ask God to help us and because sometimes we challenge, "Lord, we're drowning," that somehow we're not saintly or holy or good! No! It's only when we question whether He cares that we show our lack of faith.

Here's a good passage in Scripture that proves how much God cares, even when we're in a low ebb. It says here that after Jesus sent a demon out of a boy, the disciples came privately to Him.

(They're always coming to Him privately; they don't want anyone to know how little they understand.) They said, "Why could we not cast it out?" Jesus replied, "Because of your little faith. For truly, I say to you, if you have faith as a grain of mustard seed, you will say to this mountain, 'Move from hence to yonder place,' and it will move; and nothing will be impossible to you" (Matt. 17:19–20).

When you get so discouraged that you look at God and say, "Lord, don't You care?"—even at that point that's about the faith of a mustard seed. That's an awful lot and a little: a lot of fear and a little faith. Even with that little bit of faith, God answers and hears your prayers. Look what He did for those apostles. He corrected them but performed a miracle even in a cry of distress. And you and I can look at Peter and say, "After all you saw the Master do, why didn't you trust?"

But in your life and my life, we see the Master do many, many things. I find that in my life, no matter how many miracles He performs, today the cross seems so big that I do question whether this is going to be the first time He doesn't show up. It's an amazing thing! You say, "Why, Lord?" The answer: Because your faith must grow, and even addressing the Lord—as Peter did—is an act of faith. Despite his fear and lack of faith, he wasn't completely despairing.

We look at the Old Testament and see David lamenting. After all, he was pretty rough on the Lord. He had to trust because he had darkness. He was always running from Saul, and he had problems in his own family, and sometimes his best, well-laid plans just fell apart. We have only to look at Psalm 23. See, our reaction to our problems and our despair sometimes must be that cry of faith that says, "Lord, I don't know what You're doing, but I believe that somehow out of this mess, this tragedy, this heartache, this pain, You will bring good for me." I know you've read this psalm a million times, but let's look at it again because I think we need to find some things in it.

> The LORD is my shepherd, I shall not want;
> he makes me lie down in green pastures.
> He leads me beside still waters;
>> he restores my soul.
> He leads me in paths of righteousness
>> for his name's sake.
>
> Even though I walk through the valley of the
>> shadow of death,
>> I fear no evil;
> for thou art with me;
>> thy rod and thy staff,
>> they comfort me.
>
> Thou preparest a table before me
>> in the presence of my enemies;
> thou anointest my head with oil,
>> my cup overflows.
> Surely goodness and mercy shall follow me
>> all the days of my life;
> and I shall dwell in the house of the LORD
>> for ever.

The Lord is my Shepherd. What a beautiful act of faith to know and to understand that the only Shepherd you and I have is the Lord.

I shall not want. You may have problems and troubles and vexations and difficulties on every side, but you shall not want. You will almost starve, but you shall not want. You will never be alone.

He makes me lie down in green pastures. He leads me beside still waters. He restores my soul. Have you ever been so down and so troubled that you almost feel numb? And then something happens; the clouds lift; the sun is shining; and you know that God was there all the time, and somehow your soul is at rest.

He leads me in paths of righteousness for his name's sake. He loves you and guards you for His sake and your sake.

Even though I walk through the valley of the shadow of death . . . You know, that's the darkness of the soul, the despair that comes when you see no solution to your difficulties. That's shadow.

I fear no evil. You and I today can hardly say that because we fear everything. But the reason we as Christians don't fear, even if we're shaking inside, is because He is with us.

Thou preparest a table before me in the presence of my enemies; thou anointest my head with oil, my cup overflows. Surely goodness and kindness shall follow me all the days of my life; and I shall dwell in the house of the Lord for ever. You know, you have only to take the psalms sometimes in the midst of your cares and your tribulations and say, "Lord, restore my soul to Your presence. Set me in the right path. Let me not go either to right or to left; but let me keep my eyes on Your wisdom and Your will and Your goodness."

Yes, sometimes everything around you seems to fall apart—and how often that happens today, economically, in your family life, and where you work and in your own soul. Sometimes you feel so alone, as if nobody understands. And you know, the older you get, the more alone you feel, and that's why you must constantly keep before your mind the fact that you are especially chosen by God to be a witness, a light on top of a mountain. You're never left alone. Your faith may be a mustard seed, but it can still move that mountain because Our Lord does care. Oh, He does care. He cares so much that He bought you at a great price—the price of His Precious Blood.

And so, as you go on with your everyday life in this rat-race world, where fear encompasses you day in and day out, remember to keep your eyes on Jesus because you're special, because He loves you, because He has chosen you to be a beacon in the darkness, a light on the mountain for all men to see by. You're His chosen race, His saints. He loves you. So, clothe yourself with that compassion and patience and love and say, "Jesus, no matter what happens, no matter how difficult it is, I shall always know You care."

9

Everyday Opportunities

In our quest for holiness we think sometimes, "If I were holy, I would never cause anyone else any problems." But it takes a saint to live with a saint! Think about that. It takes a saint to live with a saint because a saint is one big pain in the neck. Saints fast, and you have to eat. They're gentle, and you blow your stack. They're smiling when everything's going wrong, and you're going to pieces. Something happens, and they say, "Praise the Lord," and you want to kill them. They have pain, and they don't take aspirin but offer it up. You see, saints are difficult to live with because they're a constant reminder of what we should be.

But then here comes that nice saint, the kind who has got faults, that Italian saint who's even-tempered: always mad. And what do we do? We write him off. He seems like a holy man, but all of a sudden he loses his temper, and we write him right off. Now, maybe he controlled himself five hundred times in a row, but that one time we saw it, and we write him off because our concept of a saint is constant perfection. But the Lord says, "A righteous man falls seven times, and rises again" (Prov. 24:16).

That was the Old Testament. In the New Testament, Jesus tells us we have to forgive "seventy times seven" times (Matt. 18:22). Can you imagine somebody doing that much to you that you would have to forgive him from morning till night? And he would have to live with your merciful, condescending attitude morning till night? You know, some people, even when they're forgiving, are absolutely obnoxious. And the worst thing you can do is to respond to someone who says, "I'm sorry" by saying, "What for?" You say that because you think you're doing him a favor, but you're not! Don't pretend he didn't do anything.

If you're a teenager and you come home at three or four o'clock in the morning, you shouldn't get mad that your dad is upset with you. If he's any kind of a man, he's going to correct you—maybe harshly—if he loves you. He might be mad at you for a week. You see, love manifests itself sometimes even in hollering. You say, "Well, I don't like that kind of love." But you must accept the way people love you. Not everybody loves alike. We have to see love in correction, especially the correction of God. "The Lord disciplines him whom he loves" (Heb. 12:6).

Imagine your soul is like a piece of tissue paper. If it gets near a very intense fire, that tissue paper will be scorched before it ever reaches the fire. You'll see it turning brown because it is not able to withstand the fire. That fire is like God: God is so powerful that our poor human nature cannot withstand the sight of Him. The Lord told Moses, "Man shall not see me and live" (Exod. 33:20). It's like being thrown into the middle of the sun. You would be totally gone.

So God, in His infinite love and His infinite mercy, prunes us. It's like taking that tissue paper and dipping it in a special water that protects it from the flame, even right in the middle of the fire. You could not even tell where it is. You would look at that fire and say, "I don't see tissue paper; I see only fire." That's what God does to you. When you have tribulations and suffering and pain from your own faults, your own weaknesses, and your neighbor's annoyances, you're forced by circumstances to be virtuous.

We have marvelous opportunities every day to choose between God, on the one hand, and the world, the flesh, and myself, on the other. I can choose God almost every moment of the day. Everywhere you go there are temptations. You don't need to fall! You have within you the power of God. And when you fall, you have within you again the mercy of God. God is so merciful that He loves us enough to prune us.

You know, pain is my constant companion, almost like a friend. But I still get uptight or nervous with it. Sometimes I say, "Lord, just give me strength for one more hour, one more day." And sometimes you feel like you're right at the top of that mountain and somebody's going to just throw you off and there's no place to go but down. Everybody reaches a point when we just call out, "Lord!" But even at that time, even when you seem to have disappointed Him, even when you know in your heart that He says, "Why are you so agitated?" and "Why do you doubt?"—even then there is in the very depths of your soul a sense of presence. And you know God is with you.

Do you know that God is with you? I wear a crucifix because I don't want to forget that God is with me. And sometimes when things get difficult, I just hold on to it. I like to hold on to Him because it tells me how much He loves me. He loved me this much. And He wants me to understand that in this position, in this intolerably painful position, He forgave. That's what it means to be saintly.

The problem with you and me is that we think to be saintly is to be without feeling, without any kind of anxiety or frustration. That's a cop-out. You make excuses for yourself. You don't want to be holy, so you come up with all these little excuses. "I don't need to be holy, you see, because I'm human." Ah, now I want to look at something about being human. It's in the Acts of the Apostles, fifteenth chapter, and we see how human the apostles were.

And after some days Paul said to Barnabas, "Come, let us return and visit the brethren in every city where we proclaimed the word of the Lord, and see how they are." And Barnabas wanted to take with them John called Mark (vv. 36–37).

Okay, so far, so good. But Paul was not in favor of taking along the very man—"John called Mark"—who has deserted them in Pamphylia and refused to share their work. Well, Paul was vivacious and had a temper! They had such a violent quarrel that they had to part company because Barnabas insisted on taking Mark and Paul insisted he wouldn't go with him (see Acts 15:39). Now, the average person excuses himself from holiness because he has a temper. But see, the Lord never promised that you would never have a temper. He never promised that after redemption you would just be a neutral, unemotional person. He does say you're going to have control. Oh, what a greater gift that is. He never promised that no one would ever hurt you. But He does promise you grace to forgive. He never promised that everybody would understand. But He does promise that you will love enough to forgive.

You know, some Christians think that to be a Christian is to be healthy, wealthy, and wise. Oh, why do you have to hide under that? Sometimes you're miserable. Sometimes you barely eke out a living. Sometimes you're sick as a dog. But the Lord uses everything for your good. And though we try to change things—and we must— sometimes we can't, and accepting that is saintliness. That's what it means to be holy. It isn't hard: You've got one thousand opportunities every day to become holy. The next time somebody does something to you that needs forgiveness, forgive quickly! As soon as it begins or after it has occurred, go on, forgive. Begin in your heart. Remember, it's merely an opportunity. Maybe if you think of your husband coming home grouchy and you want to hit him on the head with a pan, why don't you look upon it as an opportunity? Go up and smooch him instead, on his bald head. Try it! I'll bet he'll just drop over dead.

You see, we are always demanding love and forgiveness. In the Our Father, we even ask that God forgive as we forgive. Oh, wow! But if we want to be saintly, we forgive first. We forgive, and we accept people as they are. We look upon them in a self-effacing manner. Consider everyone else better than you are (see Phil. 2:1–11). It's hard to do today because we're all running around, looking for identity, trying to be on top. Everybody wants to be on top; nobody on the bottom.

That doesn't mean you have to be some kind of rug for everybody. It takes humility to stand up for truth. You hear somebody telling a dirty joke at the office, and you know it's wrong! And your conscience bothers you, but you won't say a word. In fact, maybe you give one of those funny laughs that everybody knows is false. But you don't have the guts to say, "Hey, wait a minute. If you have a filthy mind, keep it to yourself. I don't want it." Now, if you don't have the guts to say that, then you belong in that filthy place because you're afraid. You're afraid of people but not afraid of God.

I understand that it's hard to be someplace where everybody swears and you may be the only one who doesn't. Sometimes you get trapped in these situations. But you can do something. You can say to Jesus in your heart every time someone uses God's name in vain, "Jesus, I love You. Praise Your Holy Name." Say it out loud a few times. Let them laugh at you. They laughed at Paul; they laughed at Peter; they laughed at John; and Jesus promises they're going to laugh at you.

Did you ever read the Beatitudes?

Blessed are you when men hate you, and when they exclude you and revile you, and cast out your name as evil, on account of the Son of man! Rejoice in that day, and leap for joy, for behold, your reward is great in heaven; for so their fathers did to the prophets. (Luke 6:22–23)

It says right there, "leap for joy." Come on, read your Scripture. Have the guts to live it. Try it. You'll like it. Go on, your neighbor needs to know. In the world today, people are not giving enough witness to help other people see the light. You're a light on top of a mountain; you're a beacon for other men to see by. And remember—and I shall repeat it a hundred times—"You may be the only Jesus your neighbor will ever see shine."

10

Old Testament Trust

What you and I need today is Old Testament trust. The Old Testament prophets were people who went all out for God. If you go way back to Abraham, just imagine how long he had to wait for a son, with his wife nagging him all that time! When you look at all the great men of the Old Testament, you find a tremendous demand God made on them to trust to the very limit.

We all remember how Abraham was about to sacrifice his son. We look at Isaac; we look at Jacob. We look at Joseph: What a tremendous amount of trust! There he is, finding himself in a well because of the jealousy of his brothers. Where is he going to go? What did he do to deserve this? People come and take him out, and then what happens after that? He gets a job with Pharaoh and the first thing you know, he's in jail. It must have been very difficult for Joseph to see any purpose in being in jail for years. And then finally God gets him out through a dream of Pharaoh.

You see, there is uncertainty and insecurity in trust. And yet God demands that we believe without seeing. We don't know how it's going to happen; we don't even know what's going to happen; and we certainly don't know why it's happening. But trust and perseverance go together. If you don't persevere, you cannot trust because the man who stops and turns back lacks trust. The darkness and anxiety you experience is not a lack of trust; it's a part of trust. You have to let yourself go. You have to do what's ridiculous.

Let's look at Moses, since we're on the Old Testament. Moses was a man who didn't want to go to Pharaoh. He says, "Lord, I am slow of speech." The poor man stuttered. The Lord says, "Go, your brother can speak for you" (see Exod. 4:10; 14-17). But then every time he goes to Pharaoh, his people are worse off for it. First, they take away the straw, and they make them work harder, and then they take away all the privileges they had. And they're saying, "Wait a minute! You're supposed to deliver us. You're making things worse! Then he gets them into the desert, and there's no water and nothing to eat! We know how the story ends, but it took a long time and a lot of doubt and uncertainty to get there!

The Lord looks down and seems to push us to the very brink of our trust. Why is that? Because God wants to raise us to a new level of trust. So don't worry! Don't worry when everything seems to be going wrong. God is saying, "I want you to have more faith, more trust, more love." Be willing to do the ridiculous. Be willing to say, "God, it's all darkness, but just let me put my hand in Yours."

Let's look at Peter. In the tenth chapter of the Acts of the Apostles, he was looking forward to his dinner, a very human thing, and it says that "he fell into a trance." And in this ecstasy, it says, he "saw the heaven opened, and something descending, like a great sheet, let down by four corners upon the earth. In it were all kinds of animals and reptiles and birds of the air. And there came a voice to him, 'Rise, Peter; kill and eat'" (10:10–13).

Now, if you're a good Christian and you're hungry and all of a sudden you fall into an ecstasy and you see this, you might just say, "Which one first?" You know what Peter said? "No, Lord; for I have never eaten anything that is common or unclean" (Acts 10:14). God has a lot of patience, and He told Peter to eat the animals two more times, and both times Peter refused.

Look at your life and see if God has asked you to do something similar. Has God asked you to forgive someone whom you're so absolutely sure does not deserve forgiveness? See, the Lord says, "Look, I want you to take this terrible thing, and I want you to throw it out. I want you to consume it. I want you to do away with it." It takes trust, and Peter, for a moment, even after Pentecost, was afraid. He says, "No, I can't do that. I shall be unclean."

Peter was still worrying about this vision when three men came to see him. He didn't know what to do. Isn't that your problem? But you see, the same thread that we see in Elijah runs through Peter: He was uncertain and even afraid, but he never stopped. He just kept going, slowly perhaps, inching his way, but he kept going. He could not understand the vision. "The Spirit said to him, 'Behold, three men are looking for you. Rise and go down, and accompany them without hesitation; for I have sent them'" (Acts 10:19–20). He's uncertain, but he goes on.

You see, we can't always see the end of the tunnel. We can't always see the solution to our problems. In fact, some solutions to our problems will only come when we're gone. But one thing you and I can do that Elijah and Peter did is inch along and trust — because as we go along, we're increasing in faith. See, faith is darkness. Some people think that faith is to see the end, but you don't see with faith if you see the end. I can no longer hope I will be here; I am here. I no longer need faith that someone will come who has already arrived. But I must understand that the Good Lord in all His majesty and wisdom works with little people doing little things consistently and sometimes in very uncertain circumstances. But they keep going on.

And you get this in Our Lady. Do you realize how she trusted God? Do you realize that as Our Dear Lord was dying on the Cross, she had nowhere to place His dead body? Do you realize that her trust in the Father was so phenomenal that even there she waited until the Father inspired a man to say, "He can have my tomb"? What a woman! I can't thank Our Lord enough for giving me Mary. I can relate to her. She struggled. You see her struggling from the Annunciation to the end, always in there, always at a distance, looking at Jesus. She was hurt when He was hurt, counting the days, counting the hours, but never losing her trust.

Mary is a model of trust to every woman, especially today. You must trust your children to God. You must trust that somehow, no matter how wayward they are, no matter how lost they seem to be, no matter how inadequate you are to help them, to save them, to enlighten them, to teach them, that somehow God will take care if you pray. And if you pray for them especially, God will take care.

You have only to look at the birth of Jesus to see Mary's and Joseph's trust. Just imagine Mary's joy in knowing that soon her Child would be born—and suddenly they're uprooted and have to go to Bethlehem on a donkey. Can you imagine riding on a donkey, about to have a baby, for all of that time? And then you get there, and there's no place to stay. Remember, you're bearing God's Son. Those of you who are really spreading the Good News and trying to be a Christian in your job while everything is so difficult: Think of how hard it was for Mary and Joseph to have such a birth on the road with no place to go. That is a tremendous amount of trust.

And then, after the Child is born, they suddenly have to run with no tools. Joseph is a carpenter; this is all he can do. He can't go out and get money any other way. He cannot feed his family. Now he's got Mary and Jesus to worry about, and in the middle of the night, they had to run, just as they were, with no money, no tools, nothing! Just imagine! But you never hear Our Lady saying a thing. She is silent because she took the will of God in the present moment as it came to her from the Eternal Father and said, "Praise You, Lord." She didn't rebel. At the Annunciation, she said, "Be it done unto me according to Thy will" (see Luke 1:38). She never stopped saying that — never! And you and I must have that in the back of our minds when anything difficult comes along. We must say, "Lord, *fiat*. Be it done to me. I am Thy handmaid."

And then there was the time Jesus was left behind in the Temple. Mary and Joseph are going in their caravan, and Joseph thinks He's with Mary and Mary thinks He's with Joseph. In the evening they meet, and Joseph says, "Where's Jesus?" And Mary says, "I don't know. I thought He was with you." Oh, can you imagine that heartache? I'm sure those three days and nights for Mary and Joseph were absolutely phenomenal in pain and suffering.

And then when they find Him, there is another act of trust. In the Temple, He's taking and answering the doctors' questions. And finally, He turns around and sees His Mother, and she says, "Son, why have you treated us so?" You ask why, and I ask why. Don't think for a minute that because you ask why, because you question, because you doubt, because you don't understand, that you don't trust. No, because it says that when He answered Mary, saying, "Did you not know that I must be in my Father's house?," she did not understand. But she pondered this in her heart (Luke 2:48–51). She thought about it, and she trusted.

You see, trust and perseverance and doubt and anxiety and frustration all go hand in hand. I think one of Mary's secrets is that she was silent. You and I gripe a lot. We complain to ourselves; we complain to God; we complain to our neighbor. But even though we may have these questions in our minds, we don't have to voice them. You can sit in your church or your living room and say, "Lord, give me the wisdom to be still! Give me the wisdom to be quiet! Give me the wisdom to say, 'Be it done to me according to Thy will.' I don't understand; I don't know; I don't like it. But I praise Your Holy Name."

I'd like to see Mary on the day Jesus left home around the age of thirty. Can you imagine living with Jesus for thirty years, and suddenly He's gone? If you have older children who have gone off and gotten married, you know that feeling like there's a big hole in your heart. But at least you know they have a home and a family! But when Jesus left Mary, she didn't know where He'd be off to—and He didn't even know where He would lay His head. "Foxes have holes, and birds of the air have nests; but the Son of man has nowhere to lay his head" (Luke 9:58). Jesus left the house of His Mother and went out to do the mission of the Father, to save our souls, not knowing each day where He would go, where He would eat, where He would sleep. That's what you'd call trust in God's providence. And it's very difficult.

I like to think of the time that Jesus stopped at Cana just to say hello to His Mother and brought all of His Apostles to a big wedding feast. (You know, it's kind of funny that the wine ran dry after the apostles came.) These were thirsty men, and there was no more wine. What an embarrassment! And Mary tells Jesus about it, trusting that He would know what to do. And He says, essentially, "So? What's that got to do with you and me? I'm not the bridegroom; I don't belong to this family." But she was undaunted! She looked at Him, probably smiled, looked at the steward, and said, "You do whatever He tells you" (see John 2:5).

What trust she had! And then you never hear a word from her after that—but you see her. Trust made her strong. Trust gave her the ability to believe without seeing, to let herself go, to give herself totally to God, to give a real commitment of her mind—not only her life and her soul, but her reasoning and her will.

God will provide opportunities for us to grow in trust. The power of His arm will be with us because He loves us and His mercy endures forever. He is and always will be faithful to His promises.

11

Decision Points

Too many people today have ceased to make decisions. We don't even know what a decision is anymore. We're trained to think of ourselves as if we're animals, acting only on instinct. If you are operating on an instinct level, that means you do whatever you feel like doing: If you feel smoochy, you smooch; if you feel hateful, you hate! That isn't the way a human being with intelligence is supposed to be! You and I are supposed to make decisions. Our nature is made to decide, and we have free wills to do that.

Love is not a feeling. It is a decision. Jesus cannot command that we have a feeling. He can only command us to make decisions, and love is a decision. That's why so many people who lived together for thirty-five or forty years are getting separated and divorced—because some old goat is running after some young chick. I said to this one fellow, "I think you're crazy." He said, "She loves me." I said, "You're crazy. Do you know what? You're loaded; that's why she loves you."

All virtues are decisions. A Christian man has a job where he's tempted to lie and cheat and take kickbacks. Oh, I know all about kickbacks. We used to roast tons of peanuts at the monastery. One time our concessionaire changed, and the new one came to me and said, "Mother, I would love to continue giving you the peanut concession." I said, "Fine." He said, "Of course, there will be a small fee." I said, "Like what?" He said, "Well, advertising." I said, "How much?" He said, "One thousand dollars a year." I said, "No, that's a kickback. I don't pay kickbacks." (He looked at me like he didn't think nuns knew that.) He said, "If you lose our business, you won't have any business." I said, "That's all right. I don't need it. I don't want it. Look, buddy, if I'm going to Hell, it's not going to be on a peanut."

Everybody laughs at that story because they think, "Over a peanut? Why not give it to him? What's wrong with advertising? After all, your little packages are all over the stands. What's a thousand dollars when you're going to make all this profit?" But do you know what happens to you? You begin to sell your soul for a peanut! Now, you may think that's funny, but the Lord doesn't. What's the peanut in your life?

Christianity is about decisions! Are you a Christian? Well, if you are, does everybody know it? Oh, you don't want anybody to know it. You hope very few know it. Well, I can tell you one thing: If you're lying and cheating in your business and you've excused it, or if you're gossiping and tearing everybody down and you've excused it, then you no longer know truth from error or light from darkness. And you're in bad shape.

I hope I scare you to death, really. Yes, I want to talk to you about God's love. I really want you to know how much He loves you. I want you to know and realize that "though your sins are like scarlet, they shall be as white as snow" (Isa. 1:18). But some of us don't even know we have any sins. See, we don't talk about sin today. It may hurt somebody's feelings, we fear. We don't want to tell anybody that they're committing adultery because we might hurt their feelings. Well, hurt them! It's better that you hurt their feelings now than that they go all the way down—because they have no concept anymore that they can change, that they can make a decision. You have to tell them!

You're not an animal who operates on instinct. A dog wags his tail. When he sees somebody he loves, he wags his tail. When he sees a bowl of food, he wags his tail. If he doesn't like what he sees, he growls. And if he doesn't like it a lot, he'll bite. Now, look at your life. You get up in the morning, you feel like a bear, and you act like a bear. And if you feel nice, you act nice. Your poor wife doesn't know whether you love her or you don't love her because one morning you come down, you're all upset, the next morning you come down, you're all peachy. You're not making decisions! You're not saying to your soul: "My soul, I want to be like God. I want to be like Jesus. And because I want to be like Jesus, I'm not going to act the way I feel."

Now, you're thinking, "That's hypocrisy! I must act the way I feel." Do you think Jesus felt good on the Cross? Do you think He felt good as He lived His life and looked out into a crowd and saw them come after Him? Looking at people in a crowd that you're trying to lift up and knowing they are out to get you: Do you think He felt good about that? But what did He do? He still looked at them. He continued to tell them about the Father's love. He wasn't there for His own feelings.

Maybe you're a Christian because it makes you feel good. You open up the Good Book, and God speaks to you through the pages and says, "Fear not, little flock; don't be afraid" (see Luke 12:32). And you say, "Oh, how wonderful!" And you go away inspired but never transformed. Oh, let me tell you something else it says: "This is a wicked age. Your lives should redeem it" (see Eph. 5:15–20). Well, you're not redeeming anything if you're lying and cheating and stealing and gossiping and committing adultery and getting drunk every Friday night.

The reason we're not really Christian is we don't have guts. We don't want to make decisions. And you're not going to be able to tell God you didn't know, because no matter what denomination you're in, you have heard this Book from the beginning to the end a hundred times in your life. Now, maybe you weren't listening, but that's not God's fault. That's your fault. You have to get to the point in your life when you are going to decide to be a total Christian or not.

All you married people: One day you're going to get up and go down to the kitchen and your wife will have her hair in curlers that look like something from Mars. And you'll think, "I married that?!" But see, she's looking at you with a nasty look on your face, with your hair all disheveled and your bad breath, and she's thinking, "I married that?!" So you better start choosing love now, because if your love is dependent upon such petty things, bigger things will break it. He loses his job; she gets sick; lots of things happen. If you don't make decisions and you don't make them right away, it's not going to last. And then you'll say, "Oh well. You see, this is modern-day living. This is how you do it today. Married life is like an old shoe. See, it fits for a while, and then you just shake it off and get another one." And you go from one to another. But all along, you're not making decisions. You're just being moved along by feelings, instincts.

It's the same with friendship. There's nothing so beautiful as friendship. But what happens when the friend doesn't do what you want? What happens when the friend says no to you? What happens when he can no longer do something for you or he changes his opinion about something or his political party or whatever? Oh, now your friendship is suddenly cut off—because it was about feeling, not decision.

I knew a couple who weren't speaking to another couple for many years, and I said to them, "How come?" And the woman said, "I was going down the street and she looked at me and crossed over. I called her up to ask why, and she mumbled something to me, and believe me, I told her what I thought!" Okay then! So I said, "Did you ever go back and ask her what happened?" She said, "I wouldn't call her up if it was the last phone call I was going to make." So I said, "Okay. Let me call her up." So I asked about all this, and she said, "I don't know. I think she's crazy." I said, "Why?" She said, "I went to the dentist, my tooth was so sore, and my jaw was so swollen. I didn't even see her. I crossed the street to go to the drugstore. All of a sudden, I get a call. I could hardly talk, and she starts at me."

Look what happened. Somewhere along the line, this friendship was totally destroyed for rash judgment — and no decision was made to find the truth and repair the damage. See, the first woman could've said, "I wonder why? It must be something wrong" and ran over to her and asked, "Is there something wrong? Did I do something that made you cross the street?" And the second woman would have said, mouth still half numb, "Huh? What are you talking about?" And the first woman would have known the truth.

But decisions are something we don't want to make, because we act on this instinct level. We live that way. It is not hypocrisy when you act the opposite of how you feel!

Now, some Christians are popover Christians. You pop over to the enemy's kingdom, and you stay there a while, and you get comfortable there. After all, God is merciful, and He's got this long beard, and He's looking down, and He says, "Oh, that's all right. I understand. I understand." Oh, but He doesn't. And then you feel guilty, and you pop over to the light, and you're so good. Then all of a sudden, the devil's after you and the flesh is after you and the world is after you, and your friends say, "You're crazy." And then you pop over again.

I want to ask you a question. What happens if your little ticker stops beating when you're on the wrong side? Did you ever think of that? Did you ever think what would happen when you suddenly looked at God in all His glory and all His beauty and said, "Well, I thought You were merciful." You know what you were? Presumptuous. You know, the devil tried to test the Lord and tempt Him to presumption.

And he took him to Jerusalem, and set him on the pinnacle of the temple, and said to him, "If you are the Son of God, throw yourself down from here.... And Jesus answered him, "It is said, 'You shall not tempt the Lord your God.'" (Luke 4:9, 12)

When you're looking at God, don't forget that He has infinite mercy. His mercy is like the ocean. And it's tender, but don't presume on it. He also has infinite justice. You have a will so strong that you can say no even to God. And that's an awesome responsibility. And He's given you all kinds of helps. He's given you the Church; He's given you Commandments; He's given you precepts and sacraments; He's given you friends and neighbors and all kinds of things by which you can be helped to make the right decision. But it's all yours. It's your decision.

You can't say that you are a sinner because you can't help it. You can't say you drink because you can't help it, or you commit adultery because you can't help it, or anything. *You want to*. But you can take that weakness and make it into a tool that will make you holy. Don't miss the chance. Don't miss the opportunity that that temptation or weakness will give you. Every time you feel a good juicy temptation — to lie, to cheat, to steal, whatever it is — it's your will in between Heaven and God and His angels on one side and Hell and the devil and his demons on the other. And everyone's waiting. The devil's saying, "You're not going to make it. I got you. It's too good." And all of Heaven is looking. And you say, "I will not sin. I will not sin." And as Jesus tells us, "All of Heaven rejoices when one sinner repents" (see Luke 15:7).

Imagine the joy when you make a decision for Jesus, when you stand up and stand tall for the Lord. Can you imagine the exaltation in the Kingdom and the humiliation in the depths of Hell because you, a puny, insignificant sinner, said no to the enemy and yes to God? Say yes to God today. He loves you and wants you with Him in His Kingdom.

12

Subtle Persecutions

Have you ever thought of persecution? I'll bet you've thought about it in the past. You know: Christians 0, lions 10. But today the persecution is on in a very subtle way. Oh, nobody's backing you up against the wall and saying, "You can't worship," at least not in this country. But they're saying it in many other ways.

In fact, you say it to yourself. Do you know that many times during the day, you convince yourself that you cannot be a Christian because it's too hard? I never did figure out why people keep saying, "Oh, Mother, I can't be holy. You see, I'm married." Well, three cheers for you! But that has nothing to do with being holy. And that's a subtle kind of persecution.

What is a persecution, then? It's anything that prevents you from worshipping the Lord God, from letting Jesus take hold through the power of His Spirit and change your life. The daily struggle and fight to be like Jesus is a kind of persecution.

The people in your office persecute you because the first time you mention Jesus, they're going to say, "What are you? Some kind of nut?" Oh, they're good people! But when they give you that look, what happens to you? All your religion goes up in smoke! That's persecution. Remember what Jesus says in Matthew: "Blessed are you when men revile you and persecute you" (Matt. 5:11). Today, we'd run the other way or change our religion.

You say, "Oh, I would stand tall." You'd stand tall in your office if somebody mocks you because you won't listen to a dirty joke? Do you stand tall when there's gossiping? Do you find something nice to say about the person being gossiped about? Maybe you think, "Oh, this is horrible," but there is something you can do about it. You can give the gossiper hope of changing by saying, "Hey, look, none of us have any natural holiness. We're all struggling people. You have your faults; I have mine; they have theirs. Why don't we build them up!" Somebody says, "So-and-so is so nasty." And you can say, "Oh, but I've seen So-and-so be almost heroic sometimes." Now you have taken a persecution and squashed it. You have taken what might be a lie about someone and obliterated it. See, that is a fight for holiness. It's a struggle, but you can do it. You can do it by standing tall for Jesus in this world that doesn't know how to stand tall anymore.

The time is coming when we will have to cling together as a Christian community, when we will have to stand tall. Because very slowly and very subtly, the world, the flesh, and the devil are trying very hard to change your way of life, to change your mind, and to sow doubts in your heart about your Church, your priests, your community, your neighbor, your family, yourselves. There is fear, hopelessness. When you get into that state, let me tell you that if the time ever comes when you have to stand tall for Jesus, you won't; and neither will I, unless we stay very close to Him in our hearts. And when the opportunity comes, you stand tall.

"Blessed are you when men ... utter all kinds of evil against you falsely on my account." Listen to that. It's the most ridiculous thing in the world, in the eyes of men. The Lord had the audacity to stand up before thousands of people and say this to them. St. Luke's Gospel adds, "Rejoice in that day, and leap for joy" (see Luke 6:22–23). Can you imagine?

Oh, the Lord's demands in Scripture are phenomenal. He asks for your total self. We don't want to give ourselves. I love to think of that Sea of Tiberius, when the Risen Jesus told the apostles all the wrong ways to catch fish. But they listened, and they caught more than they could handle! Then it was John who said, "It is the Lord!" (John 21:7). Peter again does the dumb thing: He puts a cloak on, as if that's going to make any difference, and then jumps in the water. Poor Peter.

But what does our Lord do then with the fish? I just love this. Our Dear Lord had a fire there, and fish, and charcoal, and bread, and honey. And He made breakfast. God made breakfast. Why are you so afraid of a God Who made breakfast for His apostles? But you know, the most beautiful sentence I find in that whole passage is this: "Bring some of the fish that you have just caught" (John 21:10). Isn't that tremendous: "that *you* have just caught." Jesus told them when, how, and where, and then He put the fish in it! But that's what He said and that's exactly what they did. You see, it was all Jesus *and* all them.

This is one of the most beautiful passages of Scripture, one you should read often, because it's so encouraging. But it also tells us how deep-rooted our pride is, when we compare ourselves with Peter. And I do that a lot because pride is very subtle. It's inside our hearts, and it excuses us; it makes us feel so reasonable. If you and I were fisherman, we would have convinced Jesus it was not the right thing to do, and everyone would have missed a tremendous miracle. We would have missed seeing Jesus. The subtle evil in our lives that comes from our own pride is the hardest, because we don't see it. It looks so reasonable, so realistic, so practical.

This is what happens when you're at work, and somebody's doing something that just isn't right, and you don't say anything to him out of fear. We don't give God a chance to work. We are so afraid. We're so convinced that this cannot be done. We have shallow water. It's the wrong side of our boat. It's the wrong time of day. It's the wrong place. And so we reason ourselves out of doing what the Lord asks of us. The opportunity is over. But these apostles, for all their faults, had big hearts and were willing to let a stranger direct them in a stupid way. They were not unwilling to take risks.

You and I, though, are unwilling to take risks, and so we give up. And we say, "Well, I'm only human." What do you think these men were? Didn't they really prove how human they were? By being able to do the right thing at what seems like the wrong time, they encountered a miracle. And do you know what's especially beautiful about this? Not only did Jesus make breakfast for them: He took the bread and He broke it, as if He couldn't do enough for them. He was so excited. We don't look at God as excited over every good thing we do. But we should, because He is! God and all His angels and all His saints rejoice because you, a sinner, say, "I'm sorry."

When life gets rough with you, and people are rough, and you begin to lose hope, read this passage. After the meal, Jesus said, "Simon, son of John, do you love me more than these?" (John 21:15). Remember, Peter succumbed out of fear in his denial during the Passion. Before that, he had said to Jesus during the Last Supper, "Though they all fall away because of you, I will never fall away" (Matt. 26:33). That's pride. It's a kind of persecution from the inside that either keeps you back from doing what you should do for God and Kingdom or pushes you forward into things you are not able to do. The Lord looked at him and said, "Simon, Simon, behold, Satan demanded to have you, that he might sift you like wheat, but I have prayed for you that your faith may not fail" (Luke 22:31–32).

And so, at breakfast on the beach, Jesus asked Peter three times —three denials, three professions of faith and love—"Do you love me more than these?" And Peter, this time, is much brighter. See, there's hope! Don't get discouraged over your faults and imperfections. Even if you've goofed off, use that very thing to bring yourself up. Because the second time He said it, and the third time, Peter was now a little bit smarter—and humbler. He's learned to use the persecution within. He is not succumbing, and he's not falling beneath it. He's rising. And he says, "Lord, you know everything; you know that I love you" (John 21:17). He didn't say "more than these" this time.

In your life, you've got to give God a chance. You've got to give Jesus the opportunity to do the miraculous in your life. As I love to say: If you're not willing to do the ridiculous, God will not do the miraculous. If you can't do the ridiculous, you've convinced yourself God can't do it. How often have you prayed, and prayed very hard, and then suddenly said to the Lord, "Well, I'm not too sure You can do this. Maybe You could do it this way or that way. I'm not too sure." That's fear. Fear, when it envelops your heart, paralyzes you. It's a spiritual paralysis, and it's the hardest thing to resist because it seems so reasonable.

I am not telling you to be presumptuous or unreasonable! I am not saying that faith is unreasonable. It's the only reasonable thing around! Faith is the only reasonable thing around because it means that you are willing to do God's will no matter what anyone thinks of you. Human respect is also a very subtle persecution because it grips your heart with fear—fear that you're going to lose somebody's friendship; fear that you're going to lose your job; fear that this or that is going to happen. You're not willing to throw out your net on the wrong side of the boat, at the wrong time of day, in the wrong place.

Maybe to you it's ridiculous to stand tall for your Faith in your work situation or in your family because of ridicule. But Jesus said, "Leap for joy!" You should not be disheartened! You cannot succumb to the fear that comes from inside you at the thought of standing tall for God. And that's why many Christians today are not beacons on top of a mountain.

I wonder what would happen if someone who had never been exposed to civilization suddenly became exposed to this society — someone who never knew anything about God, Jesus, salvation. I wonder, if he were to go into a church or a Christian home, would he know by looking at us that there's something different, or would he see a lot of the same? What would he see if he looked at you and me? As a Christian, you have a mission: to radiate Jesus! You're not just some little pipsqueak that's running around. Do you think God just made you and then suddenly forgot about you among the billions of other people in the world? No!

That's a persecution, too, because the world is telling you, "You're no good. You're like an animal, so you might as well act like an animal. There is nothing to come after all this, so you better live right now. Eat, sleep, drink, and be merry, for tomorrow you die like a dog." By the time you find out the truth, my friend, it's going to be too late. The time when you're going to find out is when you see God face-to-face, and then what? Do you think the guy who told you that is going to be around? Oh, no. You and I face God alone. You're born alone, and you die alone. It's a beautiful part about being a child of God: It's all the Lord and me and my neighbor. And because your neighbor is affected by everything you do and everything you say, it's important that you understand your mission.

Don't let anyone tell you that you're not important. Don't let anyone tell you that you have no influence. That's another persecution. You can walk down the street and have influence. St. Francis of Assisi said to one of the brothers, "Brother, we're going down to the village to preach." And the brother was so happy. He stayed up all night getting his little notes ready, and he was prepared to go out there and sock it to them. And so Francis took this brother and they walked very quietly all the way through the village, turned around, walked all the way back, and didn't say a word. The brother was confused and said, "I thought we were going to preach." And Francis looked at him and said, "Brother, we did. We did preach a great sermon."

Don't forget that. That's another one of those subtle persecutions: The world says, "If you're not on top, and everybody doesn't know it, then you're not succeeding." But Jesus said, "You are in it, but you are not of it" (see John 17:16). The man may be so far on the bottom that the world doesn't know he's there. You, in a lonely apartment, can save your city, save this nation, save this world because you love God, because you're unafraid, because you trust, because you are willing to do the will of God with joy in your heart, because you are unconcerned about whether they like you or abuse you or think you're a fanatic. Who cares? Because when you die and I die, the Lord will look and say, "Well done, good and faithful servant; you have been faithful over a little, I will set you over much; enter into the joy of your master" (Matt. 25:23).

13

Reflecting God

You are destined by God to reflect His image. Did you ever go to a clear, still pond? It's hard to find one today, but if you ever do, go down and kneel at the edge of it and just lean over and look at your image. It'll be kind of wavy, but you'll see it—not perfect, but you'll know it's there. That's exactly what God has in store for you. When others see you, they must see a little ripple of the image of Jesus. Just imagine your destiny!

The responsibility that a Christian has before the world is tremendous. I want to scare you a little bit. I love to do that: I give you hope, but also I want to scare you. It says in the fourth chapter of Ephesians, "I want to urge you in the Name of the Lord not to go on living the aimless kind of life the pagans live" (see v. 17). What does it mean to have an aimless life? It means you have no goals. It means you don't know what Christianity demands. And if you don't know what Christianity demands, then you're just aimless. You go to church; you belong to that organization; you do this thing and that. But in between there are huge chunks of your life that are no good or lukewarm—aimless, without a goal. You're supposed to desire one thing if you're a Christian, and that is to be like Jesus—that the ripple in that pond will begin to straighten out, so that it is so beautiful that you can hardly tell the difference between the image and the one looking. Now you've got the idea of what it means to be a Christian.

Now, let me give you a little more of St. Paul from that part of Ephesians. He says, "Intellectually, they are in the dark" (see v. 18). How many people are in the dark today, intellectually? We reason ourselves out of everything, even sin. You don't commit adultery; you "love." Well, three cheers for you, buddy, but it's adultery! No matter how you slice it, it stinks before the Lord! Intellectually, you're in the dark. Paul continues, saying pagans are "estranged from the life of God." This means that the image in that pond is not there because you're not even looking at it. You're not looking at Jesus to have an image.

We've got to know why we were created. We were created to know Him, to love Him, to serve Him, and to be like Him so our neighbors will look at us and see Jesus. Remember, you may be the only Jesus your neighbor will ever see. And so your mission in life is great. You have great dignity and great power, and you're supposed to be a new creation, not the old man. If you're the old man inside, you're in bad shape. You don't prove that Jesus redeemed, because you're just the old guy you always were.

You know, there's every kind of difference in your family life, in your work life, in your parish life. But Jesus never asked us to be like everyone else, or everyone else like me. He just asked me to love — to love you, to love myself, to love my Church, who is a mother, Holy Mother Church. Say it sometimes to yourself. A mother is someone who's warm and kind and gentle. And a man is supposed to be like the Eternal Father: powerful and strong and provident and merciful and compassionate and loving. You're called by God to be all those beautiful things. And they're hard to come by. It's a struggle. You don't feel loving sometimes; and other times, people are hard to love, even those in your family.

But see, Jesus never promised us it would be easy. What we have, though, is joy. Remember from the Beatitudes in Luke, about being persecuted: "Leap for joy!" The world says nobody should be happy.

That's why the best way to bug your neighbor is to be happy! Be full of joy, and everybody thinks you're out of your mind. But your joy is not of this world. Your joy is in Jesus!

That's the joy of holiness. We're all called to be holy! And to be holy, you need to do two simple things. First, say "I'm sorry" often—first to God and then to your family. Be quick. Don't just *do* something that *means* "I'm sorry": Say the words. Every time you do, and really mean it, all Heaven rejoices. What a tremendous gift to be able to say "I'm sorry." And say another thing very often. Say "I love you" to your wife, to your husband. We've lost the beauty of "I love you." We think it's mushy or emotional or whatever, but the whole world needs to hear one thing, with strength and power—first, that "God loves you," then "I love you." You must say that often to your friends. This world is not starving from economic problems. It's starving from a want of love.

This world is starving for love because there aren't enough Christians in this world—perhaps in your neighborhood, perhaps in your church, perhaps in your family—who are willing to sacrifice and love. Remember, it takes great sacrifice to love. This doesn't mean you should be somehow forced to love me or to love your family or to love anybody. What we mean is that it demands being like Jesus. And looking at His image in the pond demands that you bend over—an attitude that is one of humility.

It takes humility to love. You have to understand other people; you have to put up with their eccentricities. You have to love them. You have to love them all along. You can't just look at people and decide, "I love this one; I don't love that one." And because the world is starving for love, it has a wrong concept of love. If the world doesn't find love in a Christian, it will create its own kind of love, and it will be false and selfish and painful.

But the love that Jesus is talking about is high and great and fulfilling. It isn't something that drains something out of you. It's something that puts something into you, so you can give it out! Any other kind of love drains and drains and drains. And one morning you wake up and you're an empty vessel. And nobody wants you anymore because you have nothing to give. They have drained every single bit of love out of you, and there's nothing left. Ah, but the joy and the happiness of a Christian is different because it's built on sacrifice, because it's built on Jesus, because it's called to share His love, not to just give.

But see, the Cross is something that gives, but it never runs out. The Cross represents a vertical relationship with God that's deep, and it feeds us. And then the horizontal beam, that's your neighbor. But some people run around their whole life with a horizontal bar on their shoulder and they have nothing to give, because once that's gone, they're finished, and the world just throws them off like a dog. That image that you're supposed to reflect is not there. The image is selfish, not Jesus. And so, St. Paul is saying here in Ephesians, you have to put on the new self (see 4:22–24).

Can you imagine what it would mean to be miserable one day, then to wake up the next morning feeling full of love for God and your neighbor? Can you imagine being full of fear today and waking up tomorrow full of confidence in God and in yourself? Today, looking upon the whole world as a hopeless situation that's only going to get worse, and tomorrow, knowing that it's all in the palm of His hand? Can you imagine having a temper today that you can't control and then suddenly being filled with the Spirit and saying, "Lord, look at me. I'm a new person"? Can you imagine that?

Paul says, "Your mind must be renewed by a spiritual revolution." Oh, we don't want a spiritual revolution. We're very comfortable; we're very complacent. We don't want a spiritual revolution. We don't want the Spirit. We don't want anything but a complacent life. Nobody bothers us; everybody agrees with us. Well, I don't intend to agree with you. I intend to be a thorn in your side. You know why? Because you're supposed to be a thorn in somebody else's side. You're different. You're a Christian.

What do I mean by "a thorn in somebody's side"? Well, if somebody in your office is doing something that's not right and you don't go along with it, aren't you a thorn? Every time he looks at you, his conscience bothers him. And praise God for that! Somebody in your office is so despondent all the time, and you say, "Look, the Lord's going to take care. I don't know how, I don't know when, but He's going to take care." And you go your joy-filled way, and they look at you and say, "Oh, I don't like that person being around. He's always happy." The next time you get company and they're staying too late, just talk about Jesus, talk about Heaven: Just be joyful. When they say, "Everything's going to pot," you say, "God will take care." When they start telling you all their troubles, you say, "That's all right. Have trust. The Lord is going to take care." They're going to go home. They don't want to know that they're in the hands of God. They want to know and think they're in their own hands because when they think they're in their own hands, they think they can handle it.

Oh, nobody wants to have the faith that's shaky, the faith that takes sacrifice. We must put on a new mind. We must think like Jesus. Remember the mirror in that pond: Every day, there must be fewer ripples; every day, less confusion; every day, less turmoil that makes the image blurry. That's what life is. Your whole life is looking at God in this pond until it becomes so beautiful that everybody who looks in the pond sees not you but Jesus.

14

Good and Bad Fear

We're going to talk about fear and faith: fear versus faith or fear in faith. Most people think that if you have deep faith, then you have absolutely no fear. Well, that's like saying that a man who's courageous doesn't have fear. Oh, no: The man who has absolutely no fear may be presumptuous. He may stick his head out when he should be hiding somewhere. On the battlefield, it isn't the man who runs recklessly into the middle of the field who's a good soldier. He'll get shot down. It's the man in the foxhole, shaking in his boots but persevering.

I wonder if we understand the negative aspect of faith. I shake sometimes. I'm afraid. You mustn't worry that, because you don't know what the future is, you don't have faith. Faith means that in the midst of darkness and turmoil, you know that God is there and is taking care of you. If I were in a tunnel and I had no way of seeing the end of it but something inside of me said, "There is an end; you're in the right direction," I would feel a presence. Faith and presence go together, but it doesn't do anything for my adrenaline glands! My body may react to the fear of the moment, and I could still have faith.

A lot of people think that faith is expecting God to give me whatever I want. You know and I know that sometimes you ask and ask and ask, and you get absolutely zilch. Real faith recognizes that the answer to the prayer might have been no! Did you ever think about that? Jesus said, "Whatever you ask in my name, I will do it" (John 14:14). But we can't just be name-droppers. To use His Name means to be like Jesus. That means when the Father sees you as a Christian, He sees His Son. Now you can ask in His Name, because He looks at you and He sees His Son in all His compassion, gentleness, love, and peace. He sees all that in you. Now you can ask in His Name. Don't be a name-dropper, because faith and fear sometimes do go together.

I remember when I had an operation and the doctors told me I might never walk again. I was scared. I shook in that bed, and I was petrified. But I said, "Lord, I know You'll take care." And believe me, I shook all the way to that operating room. And the Lord did take care, but you know, I had to go through a real purification period. I had to believe when I saw nothing! And that seeing nothing is scary. So don't you feel bad, and don't you think for a minute that you lack faith because you're afraid sometimes.

You know, we live in a life of pretend and fear. Nobody wants to be himself. We're always afraid; we're always keeping up with the Joneses. Your neighbor has a Buick and you want a Rolls-Royce. But all you can really afford is roller skates. We're trained from childhood to pretend and never to admit defeat, because you want to tell yourself you can do everything, and that everything you do is right and good. The only people who are always right are those in Hell. That's why they're there! They will never admit they did anything wrong. So, when you do anything wrong, say it! "I'm wrong!" Be honest.

Let's look at the story of the woman who was cured of the hemorrhage. It begins, "When Jesus went into the boat and crossed to the other side, a huge crowd gathered around Him and He stayed by the lakeside" (see Mark 5:21). Just imagine. What was it that made a crowd gather around Jesus? You know what it was? It was His love and His compassionate eyes. The eyes of Jesus looked upon you and said, "I love you. I forgive you. Come to me." You see, the Pharisees of His time and the doctors of the law were always sitting in the synagogue exhorting the people from afar. And Jesus went into their midst. We have a record of some of the things He said, but there are volumes, St. John said, that could never be written (John 21:25). What is it that could never be expressed? It's love! It's beyond words. Poets have tried through the years to put love into words, and they always fall short because love is a look; love is a touch; love is an attitude of heart and a forgiving spirit. Love grows only by loving.

Here's this woman who has had a hemorrhage for twelve years. Scripture says that she heard about Jesus. What did she hear? She heard about His compassion and His love. And do you know what she did? Just as you and I do, so afraid of God: She came up from behind Him, so unclean did she feel. For she said, "If I touch even his garments, I shall be made well." Now, we're talking about going right down to the ground. She was afraid to touch His shoulder or His elbow or His hair. She thought, "I'm not worthy. I'll touch the hem, the very bottom of His garment. And then I shall be healed." She believed that this was the Son of God. And St. Mark says, "And immediately the hemorrhage ceased; and she felt in her body that she was healed of her disease" (Mark 5:28–29).

And then here's a beautiful sentence: "And Jesus, perceiving in himself that power had gone forth from him, immediately turned about in the crowd, and said, 'Who touched my garments?'" (5:30). Can you imagine? Jesus, if you touch even the hem of His garment, loves you enough to know and to heal you. All of you who keep reaching for His hem, all of you who feel so unworthy, so little, so insignificant, the Lord calls you to rise. And He says to you, "Who touched me?"

The woman was scared because Jesus felt something leave Him. Isn't that marvelous? You know, when you spend time in a church before the Eucharist, or you kneel in your home, and your heart is broken and you're frustrated and you can't find work, and you don't know what to do or where to go next, you more than touch the hem of His garment—and the same power leaves Him and goes out to you. And though sometimes our situations don't change as we'd hope, that same power touches you. The story ends like this: "But the woman, knowing what had been done to her, came in fear and trembling and fell down before him, and told him the whole truth. And he said to her, 'Daughter, your faith has made you well; go in peace, and be healed of your disease'" (5:33-34). Isn't that marvelous?

Now, the woman didn't heal herself. Jesus healed her because she had confidence in His love. But what happens to the person who has great confidence in God's power, who says, "Lord, I know You can do this," but who isn't healed. If you are not healed, don't you let anyone tell you that you have a demon or that you lack faith. That is an evil lie. Because there's an even greater faith to be able to endure pain and say, "God, I love You." Believe me, that's faith. There is a deeper aspect of faith than being healed.

God does heal. I have seen miracles that would astound you. But the greatest miracle I have ever seen was a woman I visited in a hospital. She had cancer of the bone, one of the most painful of all diseases. She was on a bed of cotton because every time you turned around, a bone would break. And they couldn't find a place on that poor body to put a needle. There she was, and she looked at me, and I shall never forget that smile. I said, "I'm sorry that you're in such pain." And she said, "Oh, don't be sorry. You see, He had more pain. And soon, I will see Him face-to-face, and I praise His Name for every pain." I have not seen such faith in my whole life. So all of you who are not healed: You're praying, you're asking God, and you know He could heal you. You know that this particular situation could disappear tomorrow. Don't ever think, in that situation, that God doesn't love you or think you don't have faith. The faith is to believe with all your heart and all your soul that God is doing the best for you, though all seems lost. Now that's faith. That's the kind of faith that Abraham had. That's the kind of faith that Paul had.

The bad kind of fear is the fear of going against the world. I find a tremendous amount of people believing in God, but they don't stand up for their faith because their fear is of persecution, of their neighbor, of losing their job. That kind of fear prevents you from witnessing for the Lord. It prevents you from saying, "I am a Christian, and I will not stand for this." But the faith that says, "I don't know. I hope this is right. Lord, I want to do the right thing, and I'm trying to do the right thing, and I just don't see the way, but lead me." Now that kind of fear is a part of faith. You're there and you're sick in bed and you say, "Lord, I know You can heal me. I have six kids, and I've got so much to do, but I trust Your will."

You know, some people act as if saying, "God's will be done" is something evil. Where is our faith? Do you really believe God loves you? Then if you do, you know that everything that happens to you is for your good. And it isn't always a peaceful experience. You don't just wake up every morning and say, "It's such a wonderful day." Sometimes it's an absolutely rotten day, and it begins rotten when you get out of bed. And you're afraid, "If it's this rotten now, Lord, what's it going to be for the rest of the day?" Faith can be scary.

You know, at the very Resurrection of Jesus, the apostles were afraid. They had never seen anybody rise on his own. Now, they were positive this was God. They were missing Him, and yet they still said, "Oh, it can't be." He told them He would, and they couldn't fathom it. And everyone was afraid. Now Mary Magdalene, she wasn't afraid. She had a lot of love in her heart. You know, you have to admit that all the women in Scripture come out right on top. The guys are kind of shaky sometimes. That's all right, because the men had a lot of work to do. They had to be more confirmed in their faith. And because of that, they had to suffer more.

You know, Peter's faith was increased by his fall. It was his fall that made him humble. And do you know why we don't have much faith today? Because we're not humble. We don't believe that the Son of God is going to work good with the humble. We will not believe that God is going to work good in this. And if I don't believe it, then I'll be afraid of the humility Jesus calls us to. Bad fear destroys humility.

The difference is between the kind of fear that destroys you by saying, "God can't do it" and the fear that is part of faith that helps us say, "Lord, I know You can. I hope You will. But whatever You do, I want You to know that I love You and I will accept it." Faith is accepting your lot in life with great love because you believe with all your heart that God is with you and in you and will use your situation to prune you.

And, yes, that includes suffering. Suffering is a part of life. His Cross is your cross and my cross. And if we are not aware of the darkness within the cross, then we will fight it; we will pretend it's not there; and we will become bitter when it doesn't go away. But faith is that light on top of a mountain that says, "Lord, I'm a little shaky, but I know You love me and I know that You will bring good out of everything that happens to me."

15

Accepting Suffering

No one wants to hear about suffering. Why? Because we've got so much of it. But for that reason, sometimes we fake it. We live in a world of fake. Everybody pretends — to be somebody they're not, to have talents they don't possess, to have brains they don't have, to have degrees they don't have. And so sometimes, as Christians, we're so accustomed to this fake generation that we fake suffering.

I don't mean that we pretend to suffer. No: We pretend that we don't have suffering, or that it went away. We're ashamed to suffer, and we're ashamed of the Cross. We're ashamed of Jesus dying on the Cross. Oh, we don't say that. We believe He's here, and we believe He suffered and died and redeemed us. But when it comes to us, we act like He came to put us in a utopia. We're going to have health and wealth and wisdom, and everything's going to be just perfect! Aw, come off it! It isn't!

Let's get this straight: People don't suffer because they lack faith. Listen, if there's anybody who has faith, it's the guy with pain. If there's anybody who wants to get rid of it, it's the guy who's suffering. We have to have a balance in our mind between the healing power of suffering and healing itself; we have to remember the molding power of pain and suffering. Because if you don't, the enemy will convince you that it's an evil, and you'll either pretend you don't suffer or you'll think it's the enemy making you suffer.

Let's say a person gets cirrhosis of the liver because he pickled it with alcohol. He goes to the doctor, and the doctor says, "You've got cirrhosis of the liver because you drink too much. You've got to stop." And he stops. Now, what about that pain from the disease that was caused by sin? It can be redemptive! It can mold him. He can say, "Lord, I deserve this. I've brought it on myself. This is the only thing that has stopped me from drinking myself to death." If he says that, he has changed. God has healed him in his spirit and in his soul if he accepts that suffering with resignation, with love, and with deep faith, saying, "God loves me a lot. He loves me enough to stop me dead. He loves me enough to care more for my eternity than for my pleasure here."

And that goes for losing your possessions. During the Great Depression, so many people committed suicide because they lost what? Their homes? Their boats and cars? You can get more homes; you can get more cars; you can get more boats. But you have only one soul. And you either make it or you blow it. So don't fight the suffering and the pain that Jesus gives you. You pray to endure, pray to be healed, pray that it be taken away; but always with that deep humility of heart that says, "God loves me. And He loves me enough to prune me. He trusts me." God trusts you. Can you imagine that? He trusts you with pain and suffering.

The Church has taught, and shall continue to teach, that pain and suffering are either ordained or permitted by God. The Holy Father[1] has said just recently that the sick who give their sufferings to God as a holocaust in incense prevent the vengeance of God from descending upon us, because in those who suffer, the Father sees the perfect image of His Son. You may say, "Well I don't believe that. I believe God wants you healed." Yes, He does

---

[1] See Pope St. John Paul II, apostolic letter *Salvifici doloris* (February 11, 1984).

want you healed. But who is to say what kind of healing you need? Only God.

It amazes me that we, as Catholics, do not look at the lives of the saints. Look at Our Lady, that magnificent woman. Is there anyone who suffered as much as she has? Having to run from a tyrant, having your Child born in a stable, finally presenting that Child in the Temple and having the high priest say, "This Child is destined for the rise and the fall of many" (see Luke 2:34). What mother would love to hear that? Losing Him for three days, finding Him and living with Him for so many years, and then seeing Him humiliated by those who should have known Him and accepted Him and loved Him. Finally, seeing His apostles run in fear, betraying Him, denying Him. And seeing Him die on the Cross. What woman suffered as much as she? Who dares call pain evil? But our sweet Mother went through the darkness in the valley of the shadow of death for you and me over and over and over. Don't give the devil prime time. Spend your time loving Jesus, filling your heart with that faith that can touch His garment, and feel the power come to you.

That's the kind of faith that Our Dear Lord expects of us, the kind of total abandonment. We're talking about a detachment of heart and soul that says, "Lord, I am Yours, and whatever You do to me or with me or for me is okay with me." That is faith. That is confidence. This is what Our Lady did her whole life. This is also what Joseph did.

You know, it took a lot for Joseph to look and to know that this was God's Mother and God's Son, and he could not give Him a decent place to be born in. Have you ever thought of that? Some of you suffer a lot because you cannot give your families the things you want them to have. And so you're very frustrated. But look at Joseph. We just suffer because we can give our kids only roller skates when they want a Cadillac. We just suffer because we want to give our children ten times more than we had—but we had enough! We had plenty. All you need is to eat and to sleep and to have a roof over your head and some means of recreation and love.

But today we don't want to suffer; we don't want to be responsible; we don't want to sacrifice. That's why a lot of marriages go down the drain—because we don't want to suffer. We don't want the privation that's so necessary to prove love for neighbor and God. If God has to treat you like a spoiled kid, so that every time you snap your fingers, you expect Him to answer, you're not anything to be proud of. Your parents don't do that to you. Love is proved by obedience. "Holocausts and sacrifice I would not have, but the obedient heart" (see Ps. 40:6).

And don't forget, you have to be just as obedient when it comes to suffering and pain as when it comes to some big gift or intention you have. It takes a lot of guts to have pain all day long. And some of you have pain in your limbs, in your body, in your heart, in your mind, and there's no way that you can get away from it. But you can suffer with Him. This is why we have Jesus on the Cross—not because we haven't taken Him down, but because we need a reminder that in our pain and suffering, we've got Somebody with us; we've got Somebody in us; we've got Somebody holding our hand.

You're not alone. You may think you are, in that lonely apartment. You may think that your children have left you in some convalescent home. Oh no. *They* may have all left you, but don't forget Him. He was desolate and abandoned. All He had when He looked down from that Cross was His Mother, one apostle out of all those apostles and disciples, and an ex-prostitute. That's it. The rest, all of them, were enemies—doing Him in, jeering Him, right up to the last.

You say, "Oh, but Jesus suffered that for me. And so I don't have to." No: He suffered to give you an example, not to take it away. We don't understand the power of the Redemption. Before redemption, man prayed to get rid of pain; and after, he prayed to endure with joy. How much greater that is. Before redemption, we needed God to answer all our prayers to prove He blessed us; but after, we look upon the Cross and know that when He puts it upon this shoulder, He has looked upon me as a son! Before redemption, our love for God was proved by what we could give Him — the firstfruits of our land and families; but after, we give ourselves — not only the work of our hands, but our very hands. We give our hands, our heart, our mind, our soul, our body, and everything we have. How much superior that is to what we had!

And that is painful. All we do is ask God for things. How many times have you said, "Lord, I'm so grateful!" How many times have you said, "Lord, I've got plenty. Go give it to somebody else." I bet you never said that in your whole life. Selfish, that's what we all are. "Give it to me, Lord. You can forget this other guy. And if I have a superfluity, I'm going to pile it up, and then I'll enjoy it when I'm old."

But you see, there is in the future a beautiful uncertainty. Christianity is an assuring religion because we know God loves us. But in that trust is a beautiful uncertainty. I've got to trust that what happens to me is from the Lord. I've got to see Him in the present moment. If you blame every suffering on the devil, you've got a problem. You're giving the devil prime time in your life; he possesses your life, because you'll give him the credit for everything that happens to you that should cause you sacrifice, that should cause you to say, "Lord, Lord, I thank You for this opportunity to be like Your Son. I thank You for loving me enough and trusting me enough to mold me."

God knows He takes a risk by letting things happen to you, by letting suffering and pain take hold of you, by letting something happen in your family. But if He permits it, it's for your good. You may get mad at Him. You may become bitter; you may lose your faith;

you may not go to church anymore. Sometimes I look at the Lord, and I get a little angry. I say, "Lord, don't You have somebody else to pick on? Is there nobody else around today? You've got to pick on me?" That's how I talk to Him sometimes. I'm sorry about it. I feel so small when I'm finished. But I've got to get it out. He knows me.

But I'm always sorry, because I think to myself, "Angelica, wouldn't it have been wonderful if you'd looked at this whole thing and said, 'Lord, look. You're trusting me. You trust me with a cross. You trust me with a pain. I wish I'd have taken it better, and I'm determined the next time that I'm going to stand tall.'" And you know what happens? I fall again. And I get up. And we fall again, and we rise and we fall. And that's also suffering. We go to bed some nights and we look over the day and say, "Lord, I goofed the whole day, and I'm sorry. But I love You. I love You."

You know, at times like that, I have a kind of peaceful feeling in my heart because I'm miserable. There is peace in misery sometimes, when we acknowledge that we depend on the Lord. We don't want to depend on anybody. We're taught from childhood to be independent, to be self-sufficient. In the end, we're taught: you don't need God, your parents, your neighbor, anyone. Oh, are we lonely and miserable! That kind of pain God definitely does not want for us. God doesn't want us to have the kind of pain that comes from a vacuum, that is a result of fighting against Him.

But even that He uses. St. Peter says, "Since therefore Christ suffered in the flesh, arm yourselves with the same thought, for whoever has suffered in the flesh has ceased from sin, so as to live for the rest of the time in the flesh no longer by human passions but by the will of God" (1 Pet. 4:1–2). God permits us to suffer to prune us — to release us from sin so we can follow His will for the rest of our lives.

You and I have no concept of Heaven. We have no concept of what it means to see God. I can't look at the sun without going blind. My eyes are not created to see that kind of power and heat and radiation. Well, neither is my soul. So God has to purify it. Jesus came. He redeemed us. The power of His grace and His Spirit on us makes us His sons. But we have to be purified.

When you suffer, you pray. You pray that the burden is lifted. That's great. But when you don't, or when what you're asking for seems long in coming, don't question His love or His power or His providence or His wisdom. You know, He might be just a little smarter than you are. So, go on, trust Him. If He gives you the power, and He will, go on and love Him and thank Him for everything.

16

Trials and Trust

The greatest difficulties in the spiritual life are trials. We tend to think that if we love God, and He loves us, then He's going to bless us with all the good things of life. And He does! The problem lies in our definition of "good things." See, good things, to us today, are comfortable things, pleasing things, consoling things—friends, relatives, people loving us, and especially lots of money and possessions. We think that the more God loves us, the more possessions we'll acquire—and this is totally against the Gospels.

Trials are just as much a good thing as a new car or even health. You might be thinking, "Oh, no. Sickness is an evil." Well, there's certainly truth in that. But God has taught us how to bring good out of evil. You have only to look at Job, in the Old Testament. Satan went to the Lord and he said, "I see a man down there who is just and holy, but take away everything he has and he'll curse You." And the Lord said, "Go ahead, take it." And Job didn't curse the Lord, so Satan said, "He doesn't curse You because he has a good family. Take his children away and he'll curse You." And still Job didn't, and Satan said, "Now, hit his body. Make him ill, then he will curse You to Your face." And Job didn't, not at all.

Then here came Job's friends (and you and I have "Job's comforters" around us too), who told him that he must have done something terrible to deserve what had happened to him. No:

We have to be children of the New Testament. Jesus suffered His entire life. He was deprived of the very essentials and necessities of life—food, clothing, a place to lay His head, everything—and He died naked on a Cross, with nowhere even to bury His body. We cannot look at the Gospels and think for a moment that pain and suffering is only a punishment from God. If you do, you take away hope.

Trials and trust go together. We must be able to see the wisdom of God. That's what Job did. Even though, during that terrible trial, there were times when he cursed the day of his birth, he never blamed God (see Job 3). He knew that God did not punish him because of anything he did. Rather, God permitted it to glorify His power in weakness. And God does the same in your life. God looks at you, trusts you enough to give you a trial, and then gives you the grace to witness to your neighbor to the power of His wisdom.

The Lord recently gave me a trial, one of the worst I've had in my whole life. It felt as if all the sins in the whole world were suddenly placed on me. It was an unbelievably heavy burden, a weight beyond your wildest imagination, as if all seven capital sins in all the world were heaped on me as if they were mine, and God was looking straight at me. I was so frustrated and so upset in my heart. If it weren't for my beloved community of loving sisters, who would talk with me and walk with me and laugh with me, I don't think I'd have made it.

One day I remember going to the chapel, where we have the Blessed Sacrament exposed. I looked up, and it felt in my soul as if He turned away, that the sight of me was so bad. I said, "Oh, God, have mercy on me, a sinner." Then another day I got angry, and I said, "Lord, I'm trying to do all You want me to do! I'm struggling! I am a sinner! What do You want? Why me, Lord? Why me?" And then it was as if the Lord looked at me from the Blessed Sacrament, looked down with infinite compassion in His eyes, and said, "Yes. And why me?"

And I realized something: that the servant is not higher than the Master; that Jesus suffered from the tension of everyday life; that He suffered from hunger and thirst; and that He was tired, so tired. He walked everywhere He had to go. And He had to put up with apostles who could not understand the simplest parable. See, you have to realize that we are a limited people. God doesn't want you always to understand. That's the beauty of love. If you love someone very deeply, the sign of love is that you believe, that you hope, even when there are no signs that seem to merit that. Faith is not just getting what you want when you snap your fingers. Faith is to be equally content when God says no as when He says yes.

You see, contentment is something that comes from a deep realization that God's wisdom brings good out of everything. Every single thing that happens in your life, all those tragedies and trials and heartaches: Notice that those are often the times you reach out most to Jesus. God, even now in the midst of it all, brought good. We must wait for that good with joy in our hearts — not necessarily happiness. When you're suffering, you're suffering. When you feel miserable, you're miserable! You can't be happy over misery. But that joy that Jesus promised you and me, the joy that no man can take away, that joy that comes with deep union with God's will in your life: That helps us to see and to understand that God's love has permitted this or ordained it.

The Beatitudes are great blessings, and they all involve privation and the good that God brings out of it. What Jesus is telling us in those Beatitudes is to be content with the present moment. He says the poor are blessed and the gentle are blessed and the persecuted are blessed: "Live in the present moment," He is saying. "Trust me with the present moment. I know what's good for you." Then, in our daily life, we neither go to presumption nor to despair; rather, we are filled with contentment in the Lord.

So don't look upon your life as a punishment, and don't be complacent just because everything is going right. Give it to Jesus. Live in the present moment. Trust Him and say, "Lord, I trust my life to You." Ask Jesus to take away any bitterness in your heart. And you can do this by thanking Him for every trial that comes your way. Be aware of your weaknesses and say, "Lord, help me to be like You." And then you will walk the way of the present moment, with joy and contentment in His holy will.

17

The Evil of Jealousy

Jealousy began with Adam and Eve. Eve was jealous of God because He knew something she didn't: the difference between good and evil. And the enemy was jealous of Adam and Eve because they were in favor with the Father.

In the next generation, Cain killed Abel because he was jealous that God accepted Abel's sacrifice and offering and did not accept Cain's. The reason God did so is that Cain did not offer the firstfruits—the best of his work. I can imagine Cain rummaging around in a bin of cabbages and picking out the one that had the most spots on it, saying, "I'll give Him this one. Why waste a good cabbage?" There is in the heart of a jealous person insecurity to a phenomenal degree. Everything takes away from him. He never looks at anything on a positive or a generous level.

You'll find that the more jealous you are, the more selfish you are. You can't be generous if you're selfish, because everyone else around you has too much anyway, and you're not going to add to their good fortune. Jealousy makes you threatened by other people's talent, other people's position, other people's intelligence. And just like Cain and Abel, you offer fruits, and tithe like everyone else, and pray like everyone else, but you never give the best, because you feel like God has not given you the best. The jealous person is always threatened and always insecure before God and neighbor, and miserable in his heart.

The jealous person has no concept of a blessing. He doesn't bless because he doesn't understand that he shares in the goods his neighbor possesses, as brothers and sisters in the human race. You have the same Father! For instance, my sisters have talents I don't have. One is a talented artist, and I benefit from her talent because she designs all the covers of the books we publish. If I want something done, she'll just knock it right out. I bless God that she has the talent, and I share in it.

Some of you are jealous of God. If your wife or husband or children are more devout than you are — if they know God and talk about God — and you feel that they love God more than they love you — which they should! — you're jealous of God. Now you're in trouble. If your family loves God and they're enthused, don't call them fanatics; bless God for the gift, and then you share in that gift, because they're unique and you become more unique; because God is adding grace upon grace. Jesus said that "He who receives a prophet because he is a prophet shall receive a prophet's reward" (Matt. 10:41). Isn't that marvelous? If I see that you have a gift and I praise the Lord for that gift that you have, then I get the same grace and merit that you have. Jesus was giving us the solution to jealousy.

Think about Jonah, who was jealous of God's forgiveness. We all know someone we feel like we'd be surprised to find with us in Heaven, someone we'd at least like to see go to Purgatory for a hundred years or so. We all think that way at least once in a while. And so did Jonah.

Jonah had another quality that you and I have: He was afraid to do what God wanted him to do. I've got a lot of experience with that. Hardly a day passes when I don't say, "Lord, are You sure that you want this? I mean, You know, it gets shaky out here on the end of this limb." God sometimes asks each one of us to do things that are a little bit shaky. As for Jonah, he was asked by God to go to Nineveh — because there were a lot of sinners there — and to warn them that God would destroy their city. But Jonah didn't want anything to do with that, so he got on the first thing he could find that was moveable — a boat. And he thought, "Aha! I am safe from Yahweh. He will not see me!" Isn't that ridiculous?

And so a storm came up: God was after him. When you're not doing His will, He puts the screws to you every so often. We're always running from what God asks us to do, and that's what poor Jonah did. You see, the reason he didn't want to go was that he suspected that after he warned the people of Nineveh, God would pardon them anyways, and he'd look like a fool (see Jon. 4:1–3). So he knew the mercy of the Lord but was jealous of it.

Sometimes we have that same problem. It upsets us that someone who has hurt us deeply may get to Heaven. Many of us have something that happened decades ago that we cannot think about without getting very angry. We say that we simply can't forget it. Well, God is not asking you to forget. But He is asking you to accept His mercy for you and for your neighbor. When someone deliberately hurts you, there is within your heart a feeling of rebellion. But that feeling is not the point: The point is what you do with it. And what you need to do with it is give it to the Lord. Jonah should have said, "Lord, I know I'm going to go there, and I'm going to tell these people that they're going to be destroyed, and You're going to come in and forgive them. How great Thou art! And even though they may think I am a fool, Your mercy surpasses our sins."

You see, God wants to forgive you and the person who has offended you. The person who's hard to live with or who's hard to work with or who haunts your memories: All of these you must give to God.

Poor Jonah was thrown off that boat, swallowed by a whale, and thrown up on the seashore in the very city of Nineveh. Finally it dawns on him, "I'd better do what I'm told." He does it, and you know what? God did forgive them. And Jonah was so angry that he sat underneath a tree and said, "Lord God, I want to die" (see Jon. 4:3). What a terrible feeling, to be so full of desire for human respect that we would rather die than have our neighbor forgiven and make us look bad. God replied, "Do you do well to be angry?" And Jonah answered, "I do well to be angry, angry enough to die" (Jon. 4:4, 9).

Have you ever said that to God? I have. We have a hard time, God and I, sometimes. I know He's always right, but it upsets me to death sometimes. And even when I'm angry, sometimes I look at Him and say, "Lord, how come You gave us this mission, and everything goes wrong? Whose side are You on?" And I know you say to God often, "Lord, I'm working hard for my family, and it's going to pot. I work hard, and I can hardly make it." We all look at God like Jonah. And God asks each one of us, "Do you have a right to be angry because of my mercy; to be angry because a mission I give you is difficult; to be angry because it looks like it's going to pot?" Never forget, my friends, that no matter what the world looks like, God has it in the palm of His hand.

You must never forget that. No matter what happens to you, no matter what gifts or graces anyone else has, no matter how poor you are, there is in one's soul a contentment that comes from knowing that God has you and your neighbor and the world right in His heart and in the palm of His hand. And everything that happens has either been ordained by Him or permitted by Him.

We find jealousy throughout Scripture. Remember Martha and Mary? Martha looked at her sister sitting there, lovingly looking up at Jesus, absorbing all those beautiful words and counsels and admonitions, and what is she doing? She's getting the carrots ready, and the meat ready, and you can just imagine her passing by and looking at Mary with envy, and that envy begins to be hatred. She's got to blurt out something, and she says, "Lord, do you not care that my sister has left me to serve alone?" But the Lord admonished her and said, "Martha, Martha, you are anxious and troubled about many things; one thing is needful" (Luke 10:40-42).

You see, when other people's lives or talents or virtues begin to threaten us, that's the first sign we are beset by the evil of jealousy. Many of the personality clashes that go on in families and workplaces come from jealousy. Someone comes in the room and they haven't even said a word, and your hair bristles. It just bugs you to death. Jealousy has come into your heart and created insecurity in that person's presence; that person's talents or beauty or whatever suddenly puts a cloak on you.

That's what happened to Saul and David. David, just a young boy, killed Goliath, and the people were rejoicing that the war was over. And they ran through the streets saying, "Saul killed his thousands and David his ten thousands" (1 Sam. 18:7). What happened to Saul? He began to be jealous of David and to worry about him taking his power. You see, greed and selfishness and jealousy all go hand in hand. You don't mind what anybody else has — as long as they don't have as much as you.

I know that many of you don't know where the next nickel's coming from to pay your gas and your electric. Many are on Social Security and just barely make it. You eat one meal a day, and that's not very much. And then you see somebody driving a big car and eating all they can eat and throwing away food from their table, food that would nourish you and your whole family, and you get a twinge of anger. And you say, "Well, it's really injustice." And it really is. But I think there is also a twinge of jealousy. And that jealousy, my friends, will consume you because it blots out light. It keeps you from blessing your neighbor.

You see, we will share in our neighbor's goods. If I have a talent and you have a talent, we're going to share this talent, because we all share in everything that builds up the family, the neighborhood, the world, the Church — that's the Mystical Body of Christ. If you're gentle, kind, and compassionate, each member of your family shares in that. Now, if you see someone who has something and you suddenly feel a twinge of sadness, the best thing to do is to say, "Jesus, I am a jealous individual." You've got to admit it. And then say, "I want You to bless this person even more than You have." And then suddenly that resentment, that revenge, that anger begins to subside. Contentment then fills your heart, because your soul is not dependent on what other people have or don't have. That's beyond your control.

We suffer from jealousy because we refuse to believe that we are unique in the eyes of God. He looks upon each and every one of us with great love and compassion. You can't imagine in your wildest dreams how much God loves you. You can't imagine how unique you are to Him, what a beautiful individual you are. If you understood that, then nobody in this whole wide world would be able to threaten you.

Because when you're fulfilled by God, you have nothing to worry about. Imagine you're a glass of water full to the brim. But if you think, every time you see someone who has something you don't, that they have dipped a teaspoon into your glass and taken out some of your water, then you become jealous. But that's a false concept! It puts you on the defensive all the time: Everybody's offending you; everybody's hurting you; everybody's out to get you. You get a Christian persecution complex.

The best way to overcome this jealousy is to compliment your neighbor. Praise him. You might say, "Well, I don't feel like praising him. That would make me a hypocrite." But there's a difference between hypocrisy and virtue! Virtue says, "There is something wrong with my desire not to bless my neighbor, so I shall do it." Hypocrisy, on the other hand, pretends to do good while wishing evil. Evil is the purpose of any apparent good hypocrites do.

But instead you can say, "Lord, here's a person who's an artist. They don't take anything away from me. They give me the benefit of their talent. Praise You, Jesus." And you can say to the person, "I think you have a beautiful talent." In that way, you disperse the enemy and his temptations, and you suddenly become a source of blessing, because you're beginning to realize that everything your neighbor has—and everything you have—comes from God.

18

A Mission to Witness

Every Christian is a missionary. In St. John's Gospel, Jesus says, "You did not choose me. I chose you" (see John 15:16). You might think that was just the Lord talking to His apostles, but remember: Scripture is yours. You've got to read it as if God wrote it just for you.

Christ goes on: "I commission you." To be commissioned means you're given a specific thing to do for a group, for a country, for a nation: For instance, an ambassador is commissioned to go to another country and sell its people on the virtues of his home country. Well, you've got the same mission. You're supposed to be so in love with God that you can't stand it. When you're really in love with someone, you have to tell others about him. People who don't know Jesus yet have to see that enthusiasm in you.

Too many Christians don't realize they have a mission to witness. True witness isn't about condemning or condescending but about living a life of compassion and love and joy and peace, and holding your temper when you're upset at somebody, and being nice to your wife when she looks rough first thing in the morning and burns your toast.

The witness is something alive inside of you. Jesus continued, "I commission you to go and bear fruit" (see John 15:16). The fruit is your life; the witness is your life—not your mouth, not your words. It's those everyday opportunities that annoy you to death, and responding to them with compassion and love.

Christians today are a scandal to the world because we don't live what we believe! We don't have the zeal, the love, or the guts. If every Christian were real, I don't think the world would be the way it is right now. I think the example and the power of the Spirit would be so great that the whole world would change. We're afraid to be Christians; we're afraid to witness; we're afraid to step out. Our Dear Lord expects much because He has given us so much. But I think the problem is that we're afraid that, because we're human, we cannot live a life of Jesus. But that's what His grace is all about! His power is at its best in weakness (see 2 Cor. 12:9). Your mind, your heart, your soul, and your body belong to God.

I love to think of the time when there was no time. The Lord gave me an experience recently that I wrote down in a little book called *Before Time Began*. He took me and put me at that time when there was no time. And I saw nothingness. I always wondered what nothingness was because everything I see is something. And there, for the first time, I saw the void. There was only God.

One morning after Communion, it was as if God took something out of my soul and placed it on a huge sphere. And I stood there. I was able to do all my work and live my life just like usual, and yet something in me was there. I looked out and I realized that the darkness I saw was not darkness. It was different. It was a void. And every so often, I would hear this part of me cry out, "Yahweh," as if it was asking *to be*, as if it knew there was a chance it might not be. And this lasted for about two weeks.

Suddenly one day, I realized what that piece of me was. It was as if God took the thought He had of me, before time began, and placed it on a sphere and let me look at it, like a third person. The strangest experience was that, as long as part of me was on that sphere, I had no concept of being born. It was as if I were waiting for His decision about my existence. It was not mine to make. And then I realized that suddenly there were millions and billions of other thoughts like me, all waiting, all there. And I realized that there may have been eighty to ninety billion people who might be.

I saw a light. But it wasn't a light, really. It was a person—a warm, compassionate, loving light. And it began to flow over all these possible human beings. As it went from one to one, it just passed over them, and they were no more. There was the void. Their chance was gone. And suddenly, as I felt it coming toward me, I became frightened, and I thought, "Shall I be?" When I saw so many disappearing, I saw so many that He had not decided would ever be, ever! And suddenly, when the light hovered over me, I heard this gentle, loving voice say, "You shall be." And the experience was over.

Do you realize how special you are to God? Do you realize that even now, as we live in a time when there are so many billions of people on earth? And how many of them know Jesus? Not only have you been chosen to be; you have been chosen to know that Jesus is the Son of God. You have been chosen twice. What are you doing with that fantastic mission?

You have this tremendous mission from Jesus that He gave us in St. John's Gospel. "The glory which thou hast given me I have given to them, that they may be one even as we are one, I in them and thou in me, that they may become perfectly one, so that the world may know that thou hast sent me and hast loved them even as thou hast loved me" (John 17:22–23). Imagine that. You have been created by God, and you know Jesus for one reason: to prove His love to an unbelieving world, swayed by the flesh and the enemy. You are to be a witness to faith and hope and love. I don't care if you are living alone in an apartment, or if you have influence over a city, or you have influence over no one. I don't care if the world knows you or no one knows you. You belong to the Body of Christ, and, as such, you influence the whole world—know it or not, like it or not. The world will know, one day, that you were in it—by your love.

When we talk about witness and being specially chosen, we're talking about everyday humdrum living. If you're in love with God, why don't you wake up in the morning with a smile on your face? You might say, "I don't feel like smiling." Well, neither do I. In fact, I find smiling painful. One day, we had a bunch of visitors come to pray in the chapel, and all day long I was smiling. By evening, my ears were sore because I was smiling all day. See, even when you smile, it's a pain in the neck. But you've got to put forth that effort that says, "Hey, I love you." I know it's difficult sometimes. We shouldn't feel bad because it's hard to love, because we're hard to love sometimes. That's life, and that's a part of holiness.

Think about going to a restaurant. (Remember, holiness is wherever you are!) So you get your seat, and you wait and you wait and you wait. The waitress finally comes, and what does she bring? Water, and nothing else — not even any chitchat. You may want to pour it on her head because you've already waited twenty minutes, but you should say "thank you"! Then she brings the menu. You read it over, she finally comes back, takes your order, and then seemingly drops dead, because she never returns. She's busy about many things — everybody else's table but yours. "You mean I have to just sit there while this screwball goes around to everybody else's table?" Yes! That's an opportunity for you to witness. See, there may be somebody in a corner who's watching you and saying, "Gosh, can you imagine that waitress? She practically ignored that table, and they're patient and happy. I wonder if they're Christian."

Christianity is a living witness of heroic virtue. You can be different from a hundred other people in that restaurant who may be just boiling over with anger. That waitress may have had a heartache or some great tragedy on her mind. She may have been very lonely. She could have been struggling in many ways that you'll never know. Somebody has to break that vicious circle, and maybe that somebody is you.

Maybe in your family right now, life is in a terrible, quarrelsome, dissenting rut. Everybody comes home and complains about the food. It's just one terrible situation, night after night after night. And you're waiting for everybody else to change. You're really not acting like you're specially chosen. You're not acting like Christianity was part of your bones. You're not acting like you're in love with God, with Jesus. You're acting like you've lost your first love.

The Lord knows how much we suffer. He knows how anxious we are in our poverty and all those frustrations that are part of our lives. He knows all that. But still, He expects a lot from us. He expects Himself to be the most important thing in our lives.

I'm afraid some of us as Christians can't say that. And so we're a scandal to our neighbor. Our neighbor does not see anything he wants in his life in how we live ours, because we've lost the realization of being specially chosen, of having a mission of witnessing to the world, of changing our human existence and lifting it up. And all of this is because we have forgotten how to love. Whether you like it or not, you and I are going to have to make an account to God of how we loved Him and loved others. Don't forget how special you are. Don't forget your mission, and don't forget to love much.

19

Taking the Next Step

Trust can be difficult to understand and difficult to practice. There is with trust a negative element that almost makes you miserable before you can practice it. Faith and trust go together. Trust says, "God will do it," when everything in sight says, "No, this is not going to happen." Trust says, even when you don't see anything happening, "God will take care. He will answer my prayers. He may say no, but He will answer my prayers." Trust says your body is filled with pain, but God would not permit it unless there was something good in it.

Trust and faith go together in a most beautiful way, and yet our lives are beset with anxiety and frustration, and sometimes when we're feeling those struggles, we say, "Well, it must be that I have no faith. I have no trust." No: You must recognize that those feelings of frustration and anxiety and doubt can be part of truth; they can take your trust to a higher level. The centurion from Matthew's Gospel had that kind of trust. He went to the Lord and said his servant was ill, and the Lord answered that He'd come and heal him. But the centurion responded, "Lord, I am not worthy to have you come under my roof; but only say the word, and my servant will be healed." And the Lord responded, "I haven't found this kind of faith, this kind of trust, in all of Israel" (see Matt. 8:8–10). The centurion felt inadequate and unworthy, but he trusted anyway.

Even where his faith was at a high level, there was a negative element to it.

Most of us think that loving God and worshipping God and praying to God entail a kind of constant joy — and they do, joy in the heart. But you cannot take away the negative aspect of trust. You cannot take away the struggle. We grow in holiness by inching along, step by step, and sometimes we crawl, and sometimes we sit still, and sometimes we're rebellious, and sometimes we think it's not worth it all. But at all of these times, as we inch along, there is a beautiful opportunity to trust and to say, "Jesus is going to bring good out of this. Jesus is going to help me. Jesus is helping me. Jesus is my strength. Jesus is my rock. I trust His wisdom; I trust His will in my life."

Let's look at Elijah, one of my favorite prophets. He was, in my mind at least, a short, scrawny, caustic little man with a temper. One time he got all the pagan prophets together and said to them, "Why don't you fellows get a bull." This was a time when it hadn't rained for three years, and he wanted to show them the powerlessness of their gods. "We're going to have a sacrifice. We're going to cut this thing in half and we're going to put a piece on your altar and a piece on my altar. I want you to call down fire from your gods." And so they tried, and they danced, and they did all kinds of crazy things. And he was there looking at them, saying, "Ha, ha, ha. Why don't you shout a little louder? Maybe your gods fell asleep." And at that moment, the Lord gave him fantastic courage, and he took the bull on his altar, put water around it, and said, "Lord Yahweh, prove to the people You are the only God." And fire came down and consumed the offering (see 1 Kings 18:20–40).

Then Elijah looked at all these forty prophets, and he told the people of Israel to kill them. And they did. But Jezebel, the pagan queen, said, "Aha. Let it be done to me if by sunset the same isn't done to you" (see 1 Kings 19:2). What does Elijah do?

He runs. Suddenly the courage is gone! He gets discouraged, and he goes underneath a tree and says, "Lord, let me die. I've had it. I've done Your will. I've destroyed those pagan prophets; now they're after me" (see 19:4). Isn't that how you feel sometimes? You were so happy before you became a real Christian, but now people call you a nut for saying things like, "Praise God. Praise the Lord." It was easier before the glorious opportunity to profess your faith before men.

You and I live in a time where we are being asked by God to confess before the world what we believe. What an opportunity! Some people will call you a fanatic. That's all right. That's what the Bible's all about. It's full of fanatics—people who talked about nothing but the Lord! You'd think there was nothing else to talk about. But they loved God, and so they couldn't stop talking about Him.

Well, here's Elijah, and he's committed, but it gets him into trouble. And now he's totally discouraged. But God sends an angel to him who offers him food, saying, "Get up and eat. You've got a long way to go, brother" (see 19:7). And on the strength of two little meals and a little bit of water, Elijah walked forty days and forty nights farther away from Jezebel. That's a lot of fear.

Finally, Elijah gets to Mount Horeb, where he was supposed to go to meet God. Then, all of a sudden, an earthquake comes. Not only was he scared to death getting there, but now he's scared to death when he finally made it! Elijah hides in a cave, shivering with fear—fear just like we have. Isn't it something that God has to almost scare us to death before we listen? Isn't it true in your heart that sometimes only in a tragedy, in a heartache, in a disappointment, in some hurt, that you finally get to know Jesus, that you finally begin to understand the reality of God in your life.

A thread that runs through the life of Elijah is trust. We have to differentiate between our feelings and trust. Feeling afraid or even questioning does not necessarily mean we don't trust. In Elijah we see someone scared, looking back, wondering if Jezebel's people are going to catch up to him — but *moving forward*. Isn't that what you do? Maybe your children aren't what you think they should be; maybe they've strayed from God, from you, from the fold. But don't ever stop loving or praying. Maybe you've been hurt in your life and you say, "I don't see any purpose to this." Or you say, "If I hadn't made this move, I wouldn't have gotten into all this trouble." Oh, come on. Don't flatter yourself. Maybe if you would have made the other move, you'd be much worse off!

That's where trust comes in your life. I can be full of fears; I am often full of fears. This apostolate sometimes scares me to death because it's so gigantic, and we're so very small. But if we keep moving ahead — just like you do, just like Elijah did. And you'll see this moving ahead in all the apostles, and you'll find the same result, because when Elijah finally moved, he got to Mount Horeb. Finally, when he distrusted himself and had nothing else but God to trust in, he felt and heard a gentle breeze. And he said, "It is the Lord." You see, that problem you have in your life, that heartache in your life, that struggle in your life: Sometimes it's purifying. It's the only thing that makes you realize how much you depend on God. And then we really begin. You say, "Well, Lord, I can't do it." But Elijah found God when he was in a state of total fear and frustration. And what did the Lord say to him? "What are you doing here, Elijah?" (19:13). Oh man, what a question after that long walk! Poor Elijah just answered, "Lord, I'm the only one left of all your prophets. And I wish I would die. I mean everything I have done was a total flop" (see 19:14).

Did you ever feel that way? Sure, that's part of life. Sometimes you work so hard, you can hardly move another bone, and it looks like it was for absolutely nothing. You know what the Lord did to Elijah? Oh, God has a sense of humor. He says to him, "Look buddy, I've got news for you. There are nine thousand that have not knelt to Baal," the pagan god. Elijah thinks he's the only faithful one, but he's humiliated again! And then the Lord really puts the screws to him. "Elijah, go back" (see 19:15–18). It took Elijah a long time to understand that God's wisdom was above his own.

The opportunities that God gives us to trust make us understand the difference between God's wisdom and our own. St. Paul says, "We are afflicted in every way, but not crushed; perplexed, but not driven to despair; persecuted, but not forsaken; struck down, but not destroyed" (2 Cor. 4:8–9). There is nothing like persecution to make you feel that God has left you alone. People are after you because you love Him, because you're trying to do something for Him and His Kingdom. And then, suddenly, you get it on every side, and you begin to wonder: "I'm alone. Not even God is with me." But Paul says, "No, we're never deserted."

A member of my crew has a nice little saying. When she's in a slump, she says that she's on "valley duty." We're like the apostles at the Transfiguration, where everything is so wonderful and everything is going well. We say, "Lord, let's pitch three tents. Let's not let any of this consolation leave us. Don't ever let me get sick. Don't let anything happen to my family—no crosses, no tragedies, no sickness, nothing. And then I'll love You and I'll trust You." That's ridiculous, see? You've got to come down from that mountain and get right down in the valley, where you don't see a thing on the other side.

When God asks you to have "valley duty," when He says it's time to go in the Garden of Gethsemane, and you look around and all is darkness and you don't see the end of the tunnel, know that Jesus is in your heart. Jesus is holding your hands. Jesus is in front of you and behind you. And though you think you're just inching along, and though you think nothing is happening, you can be sure that to those who love God, all things—all anxieties, tragedies, and heartaches—tend to good. Trust Him, will you? He loves you. And you love Him.

20

Four Stages of Prayer

Recently, I went with a friend of mine to a bank. And she drove up, got out of the car, and, instead of going inside, she went to a little window. And I thought, "What is she going there for?" She takes a card and slips it in the little slot and starts punching some keys, and I watched with utter amazement as I saw some dollar bills come out of the machine. And I thought, "Isn't that clever!"

You know, that's a good image of how some people pray. Every so often, when you're in need—like my friend needed some cash—every time you need a favor from God, you go to an automated teller that you call "prayer," and you punch a few keys, and you say to God, "Lord God, I want this." And then you stand back and wait, just like she did.

When we do that with God, it shows a lack of humility. So often, when we pray to God, we forget that He is Father—and that we are children, no matter how old you are or who you are. When you pray, you must pray as a child to a Father, a Father Who knows best.

You must have a rapport with God. You know, if I get a new pair of shoes, I go and show them to the Lord. Of course, it's easy for me to do that because we have the Blessed Sacrament exposed in our monastery chapel. And I run in there, and I say, "Hey, Lord. Look at my shoes! Thanks a million." He gave me these shoes. Now, you can do that in your home. You might say, "Now,

Mother, come on." But when you love God, He has to be a part of everything in your life.

Did you ever pray for a parking place? If you find a parking place right smack in front of a doctor's office, it's near a miracle. I've heard people say, "Mother, I wouldn't pray for parking places. I wouldn't pray for this or pray for that." You pray for sunshine and pray for rain. Pray for little things, because little things say, "I love You." Little things say to God that you trust Him because you're worth a lot to God.

God created all of this tremendous world we live in, and there's so much of everything—so many species of pears and apples and oranges. He could have made one apple, one pear, and one orange. Now, if He did all that without your asking, imagine what He will do for you when you ask with faith and hope—and most of all, when you ask with love, as a child speaks from his heart.

Jesus wants us to be simple. Don't get so sophisticated with the Lord. He knows what you're made of. You know, so many of us talk to God as if we just met Him, not as a child speaks to a Father. Now, you may laugh because I say, "Hi, God. Are You hot up there on the altar?" But He is up there, and it is hot. But you see, you must have a human and a divine relationship with God. You must be awed at His grandeur and grateful that He created you, even though sometimes you feel like you have a miserable life. But still, you must have that kind of childlikeness that says to the Father, "Look, I'm in trouble, and You're not helping out much." But it's always with a humble heart—not arrogant, not presumptuous.

Presumption is very common today. We say to God, "Look, we've asked for this in Your Holy Name, and so that's it. I want it." And if you don't get it, you pretend you do. Oh boy, why are you excusing God? If you don't have it, you don't have it. It's like eating beans and pretending it's chicken. Beans are beans, my friend. They're never chicken. If God has said no to you, don't think He doesn't love you. He loves you more because He trusts you. I always think, when God says no to me, that He loves me more than the one He says yes to, because He trusts me to continue loving Him after He says no.

You know, the Lord said we should love Him with all our heart, with all our mind, with all our strength, and with all our soul. That's your whole person. But that's also how you pray. How do you pray to God with your strength? The Lord showed me there are four degrees of prayer. The first is the prayer of strength. This is when you just begin to know that God is your Father, and you've got that vacuum in your heart. Some of us have that vacuum in our hearts right now: They're full of sin, full of anxieties, full of frustrations. When we pray from this situation, it's beautiful, because that's the prayer of strength. God is looking at your weakness and saying, "Come up, friend. Come up." You should be going to Mass and making visits so that the Lord can speak to your heart in the Blessed Sacrament. And even in your living room, you can say, "Lord, I'm a miserable sinner. I want to repent. I want to overcome this weakness." And then you will begin to feel that strength coming into your heart.

And then, once you repent, comes the prayer of the heart. We have a lot of the prayer of the heart today. Some people never go to the next step because they're always at the level of the heart. Everything is love, and everything is song, and everything is music. And if anything happens in their life that is not right, they pretend it didn't happen. But the real prayer of the heart looks at God with a humble heart and says, "Lord, whatever You say. I love You enough to take all the yesses and all the nos." That prayer of the heart means that you have deep commitment to live a Christian life, no matter what temptations, no matter what obstacles, no matter what anything. Why? Because the heart gives motivation to the mind.

This leads you to the next step in prayer—what I call the prayer of the mind, where you begin to examine yourself. This is where dryness comes in. Dryness is that empty feeling where you say, "God's far away, and He's not listening. I just don't feel like doing anything." Did you ever feel that way? That's a good sign, because it's an invitation: "Come up higher." It makes you examine your conscience. Some of us just want to push all that dirt under the carpet. But see, then there's a hump, and everybody sees the hump. The prayer of the mind is when you examine yourself and say, "You know, I have a deep hatred for So-and-so. And God doesn't like that. God forgives me, so I must forgive." And then you right away go and forgive. Or you have a resentment toward someone, or maybe you have guilt. God has forgiven you, but you haven't forgiven yourself. Now, that is the prayer of the mind, where you begin to dig in your own conscience and get rid of all the junk. Sometimes our minds are like cluttered attics.

And then comes that next step in prayer, the prayer of the soul, when you feel in your heart that very deep presence of God. You're aware of God's presence around you; you're aware of God's presence within you; and you're aware of God's presence in your neighbor. And you see, then, it's the Father in you loving Jesus in your neighbor. And that's the highest form of prayer because it's unceasing. There's always a neighbor around; there's always the world around; you're always around; so there's always a Jesus to love. And, of course, there's always a Father to raise your mind and heart to. When you get to that type of prayer, you're getting to a type of prayer that is so much a part of you that you're almost in a constant state of prayer because God, in His creation, from billions of people who might have been, chose you to be. And you are of more worth to God than all His creation.

21

The Scraps of Our Lives

One of the problems today is that so many people have real hang-ups over their past faults, weaknesses, and sins. We feel bad about what we've done, but this sorrow doesn't bring out any type of real repentance—the kind that comes from the depths of the soul. It mostly comes from a surprise that we could have done such a thing to begin with, or that we could be so immoral or so angry or so hateful. And suddenly, when we find Jesus and begin to look at our past, and it looks horrible, we're sorry. But some of the sorrow we have is not because we offended God but because we just can't accept the fact that we did it.

This kind of false humility can be very discouraging. But real humility is not discouraging. It builds hope. If you have the kind of repentance and sorrow that discourages you, then there's something wrong with your repentance. You're not so much sorry that you offended God as you are that you might be the type of person who did what you did. You have such a high opinion of yourself that you just can't imagine it—and that's where you don't forgive yourself.

And so you must understand that when you are repentant, you must begin at that moment to say, "Yes, I did those things, and I am capable of doing this again. But the grace of God in me is more powerful than my weakness." When Jesus said to St. Paul that His power is at its best in weakness, that doesn't mean that you continue in your weakness, just waiting around; God's power is not really working there. But God's power is at its best when you are overcoming yourself—not living in the past, but seeing how God uses all the scraps in your life.

That's what they are: things you want to push under a rug, things you wish nobody knew, things you wish you'd never done and could forget. Well now, you have to look at this mess and say, "Wait a minute." From this garbage, from these ashes, can come great holiness of life, a transformation—so much so that people will look at you and get courage for their own lives. That's the beauty of repentance. It gives courage to other people who are in such a condition as sinners that they don't think they can rise above it; so they just lie there, in a mudhole. But they don't have to lie there. You know what the Scripture says: "Though your sins are like scarlet, they shall be as white as snow" (Isa. 1:18). That's the glory of God's mercy and forgiveness. Let's look at the miracle of the loaves and the fishes. It says, "Looking up, Jesus saw the crowds approaching, and He said to Philip, 'Where can we buy bread for these people to eat?'" (see John 6:5). He only said that to test him, and Philip said exactly what you and I would say! He said, "Two hundred denarii would not be enough to get a small piece for everyone." He considered what he had, compared it with what was needed, and it came out zero. That's exactly what we do today. We look at the economy, the country, all our failures, our own personal lives, and we come out with zero.

And so we talk Our Lord out of things. We explain to Him (as if He needs anything explained to Him), "Lord, You can't do this. You see, it's illogical." We talk ourselves out of anything and everything, and that's exactly what the apostles did. Our Lord didn't pay any attention to them and simply had them tell the five thousand to sit down. "Jesus then took the loaves, and when he had given thanks, he distributed them to those who were seated"

(John 6:11). You know, the action of sitting down makes one very helpless. Jesus wanted them to sit, to realize their dependence on Him. They were as far as they could go, hungry and ready.

Do you see the beauty of the trials and sufferings in your life? Even your frailties and your weaknesses, they make you stand ready. And here is the most beautiful part of all. After they had all eaten, Jesus said to the apostles, "Pick up the scraps." Now, don't forget there was tall grass there: This wouldn't have been easy. You and I would've just pulled up the grass and said, "Now, that'll be good fertilizer." But the apostles, they ate that fish and bread for days afterward.

The apostles, at the direction of Christ, consumed the scraps — the parts you and I would like to have buried and forgotten about. Isn't that like your sins and your past? Isn't all that scrap something you want to bury? Isn't it something that you wish never happened? You want to pull all that beautiful grass that looks lush. You don't see all that smelly fertilizer on the bottom of it. But Jesus said, "That scrap is good. I'll make it good. It'll be nourishing."

What was it that made Peter a humble man? Was it only the gift of Pentecost? No! It was his repentance after his denial. "Once thou art converted," Jesus said to him, "convert thy brother" (see Luke 22:32). It is only the sinner who has compassion on other sinners. It is only the struggling saint who has compassion and love for those who don't make it, those who fall. It is only the man who has been forgiven much who can, in turn, forgive his brother. It is only the one who is frustrated and worried and tense who can understand. It's only the sick and those wracked in pain who can understand the sick. We all understand joy and success. God, in His infinite love and mercy, enables us all to be pruned, purified.

You know, one of the problems in our spiritual life today, besides hiding the scraps, is that sometimes, because we are sinners, we lose compassion for our neighbor. We tend to spew out the hatred — the *self-hatred* — that we have on our enemy. And you will find people condemning others for the weaknesses they have themselves. You find in yourself what you find in other people; you have to know what's inside of you to see it in someone else. A thief suspects everybody.

It was Peter's denial that brought about his conversion. Jesus did not want Peter to deny Him, but He knew his weakness. He knew he would be put to the test and fail. But God used that scrap. That scrap in Peter's life was the most beautiful thing that happened to him. He became compassionate.

One of the main reasons our repentance can be false is when it's geared toward self-pity. Some of us are in such a wallow of self-pity that we can't get out of it. All we think about is what we did, what we are, and God never enters into the picture. Peter never forgot he denied Our Lord. Paul never forgot he was a persecutor. But they didn't wallow; they used it. These men sat ready. They were vulnerable all their lives.

God is so gracious and so lavish, but He's also frugal. He doesn't want you to waste anything, even your past, even your sins. That's what humility is. Humility is the ability to accept and face the truth. And the truth may be that you were pretty rotten. That's it! It's a real bummer, but now you know truth. You know Jesus. You have experienced forgiveness. Now, can you imagine when another sinner looks at you and sees that you are happy, sees that you have been able to accept Jesus into your heart, sees that the mercy of God is flowing through you, sees that your life is transformed? He looks at you and says, "Why, I could do that. I mean, why can't I repent? I'm not completely lost."

Don't ever let anyone around you, much less the devil, inspire you to think that you're lost, that you're beyond redemption. Oh, that's bad. One of the greatest things the Spirit did for you when you were baptized was to instill in your memory the virtue of hope.

Hope is that fantastic virtue that says, "God will do what He promised; He wants me to take every part of my life and turn it around." But you've got to help God. You can't sit there and say, "Oh, Lord, pour it on me." He's not going to pour it on you. He's going to give you light; He's going to give you inspiration.

Those thoughts that come to you — "Why don't you go and tell God you're sorry? Why don't you tell your neighbor you're sorry?" — that's not you. That's the Spirit! That's your angel, and he's inspiring you! Don't push it aside. We push all these things aside as if they were our imagination. No, God is working on us. He's saying to us, "Repent," in a very gentle way. He wants you to be sorry only so you can rise and see a new light.

If you have your head down all the time, what do you see? Ground, mud. If you're looking inside yourself all the time, you're going to see mud. But you can raise your eyes and your heart to God and know that when trials come your way, they are meant to prune you. You can't say, "God is punishing me." Oh, come on. God has more to do than run around hitting you on the head. You punish yourself. If you drink two quarts of vodka, you can't blame God for a headache. You brought on the headache. But that headache could be redemptive for you! You can say, "Lord, I did this. It's my fault. I thank You because it's telling me something," as your head is pounding. Why lower yourself to this level? Rise!

That's acceptance. It's acceptance of yourself but with determination that you are not only going to change but that you can and will begin to live a deeply spiritual life with Jesus so that you are transformed. Then somebody who sees you, knowing your past, will say, "Oh, what has happened? This man has been transformed." The angry man is gentle. The drinking man no longer drinks. The dope addict has more joy than he ever had taking pills. All this because he's not afraid to be vulnerable in the arms of Jesus. He's not afraid to be repentant and humble of heart, because he knows the graces and the love of Jesus pouring into his heart.

It's just like a snowball running down the mountain. It just takes more and more within its arms, and more people and more people are transformed. Trusting the Lord is difficult. It takes humility. But see, it's the scraps in your life that make you humble. And when you're humble, you know that God's will is above your own, and that somehow He will use those scraps to transform you into the image of Jesus.

22

Healing Our Memory

We all have a favorite enemy. In your memory, you have someone or something that is like a security blanket that you love, and it's evil. It's bad news! In your memory there are shelves, just like a storehouse. And you have little jars that go back to when you were three years old, including a favorite jar. You take that jar out, and you open it, and it's just an awful memory. And yet, you're secure when you're thinking about this terrible thing. It gives you a lot of self-pity and makes you feel that you have a right to revenge, a right to hate.

You see, when we are asked by God to be holy, part of what He's saying is, "Clean up your memory. Take away those resentments. Throw them out. Clean house." You have to clean house. You have to ask yourself a question: "Is this how I'm going to gain eternal life?"

This brings to mind the Gospel story of the wealthy young man who said to the Lord, "Lord, tell me. How can I enter the Kingdom?" (see Matt. 19:16). And the disciples are looking at this man who has everything and were wondering, "What's he talking about? What else does he want?" And the Lord said, "If you wish to enter the Kingdom, keep the Commandments." But the man responded, "I've done all of this." So Jesus goes on: "If you would be perfect, go, sell what you possess and give to the poor, and you will have treasure in heaven; and come, follow me" (19:21). And of course, we know that this man, being very wealthy, couldn't do that. And so he walked away sad.

Now, we only think about giving away our possessions. But what about that old nasty memory that gives you security? You're afraid to free yourself. You're afraid because you think this favorite enemy, this terrible thing that possesses your life, gives you something that you need. You know, some people are more comfortable in fear because they've lived in it so long, they have forgotten that perfect love casts out all our fear. Some people would rather stay the way they are — miserable, hateful, obnoxious — than ever give that up.

Do you remember the day Our Dear Lord went to the Gerasenes, and there was a demented demoniac? The man was so crazed that the people would hide and bolt their doors and windows, and the kids couldn't go outside. The whole village was scared to death. And Jesus comes and looks at this demoniac from a distance. He begins to say, "Come out of him," and the demoniac rushes to the Lord, and the demon in him says, "Let me alone! What do You want from me?" The Lord looked at him and said, "Get out of him. What is your name?" And they said, "Legion." A legion of demons in one man! Jesus commanded them again to leave, and they said, "Please, send us into these pigs. Do not send us down into the lower regions." And He says, "Go" (see Mark 5:1–13).

There were about two thousand pigs there being kept by swine herdsmen for perhaps two or three hundred families, and when the demons entered them, they ran into the lake and drowned. And so the people ran to Jesus and "implored Him to leave" (see 5:17). Can you imagine telling the Son of God to leave over a few pigs? They didn't realize that now they could go out at night; now their children were safe; now they could leave their doors open. And all it cost was some pigs.

Are you sure that the pet gripe you have—the pet reason you have for not being compassionate and forgiving—is not similar to pigs? Are we not preferring hatred and resentment and regrets? Are we not saying, "Lord, leave me. I want to nourish this anger. I have a right." We're not talking about our rights. We're not saying that we have not been offended over and over, and unjustly. That is not the question. He knows that we've been treated unfairly. The question is: "How can I forgive?" He doesn't ask us to forget it, although that would be sublime. Sometimes it burns in your memory. Sometimes people ask me, "What do I do? I want to forgive, but it keeps coming back." Don't worry about it. If you want to forgive, you have forgiven. Just say, "Jesus, I give this whole thing to You. I don't understand."

One of the greatest evils in our life is that as soon as someone offends us or commits a fault, especially if the person is a Christian, we immediately begin to dislike the person. We cannot distinguish between the sin and the sinner. This is what Jesus was referring to when He told us not to judge. When you hate the sinner, you are judging that his actions were deliberate and malicious. But, really, most people don't know what they're doing. It's not that they don't sin. People make very, very strong choices. They prefer God sometimes, but most of the time, they prefer themselves and evil to God. But even then, I have no right to judge. I cannot judge their grace; I cannot judge their light; I cannot judge their weaknesses.

Compassion is a transforming virtue. It makes you like God. What did Jesus say? "Be merciful, even as your Father is merciful" (Luke 6:36). Compassion and mercy are why Jesus chose you and me to be. Sometimes we are almost jealous of God's compassion. We want our enemies to suffer. Remember the conversion of St. Matthew, the tax collector despised by the people. You've got some favorite person or people you despise. Think of them now. Now think about the Lord God coming down and being very nice to them. What happens inside of you at the very thought?

We hold on to resentments because truth sometimes will trip you up. Not the truth of Jesus; not the revelations of God: They will never trip you up. But the fact that you were really and unjustly offended by someone—that's a truth, isn't it? Someone cheats you out of money, out of your business. And it's a truth. Then that truth gives you, in your mind, the right to hate and to judge. We are very ready to condemn. I'll bet if you were asked at this moment to make up a list of your neighbors' sins, weaknesses, and faults, without blinking an eyelash you'd have a long list. But if I were to have you tell me something beautiful about your neighbor, even your family, you have to admit that the list of faults comes much more quickly. We need to focus on the beautiful qualities that the Father and the Son have planted in their souls. Compassion heals. Compassion makes things grow. It makes a flower grow out of a garbage heap. It makes things that are desolate bloom.

What are we afraid of? We're afraid of the demands of compassion. To be compassionate is to forget yourself. To be compassionate is to think more of your neighbor. It is to say to your neighbor, "Look, I know you have weaknesses; I know you have faults. I know you did me in, but I, too, am a sinner. I have done other things that nobody has ever seen or knows about." We all have skeletons in our closets. And when you condemn your neighbor, you better open up that closet and look at that skeleton; because if you don't, you're going to develop a spiritual superiority complex.

Spiritual pride is worse than any other kind of pride. Jesus was particularly upset about it. The Pharisees said that Jesus broke the Sabbath by healing a man with a withered hand (see Mark 3:1–6). That's spiritual pride. They missed the whole point of God's compassion. And we miss the point of God permitting an unjust situation in our lives. Nothing God permits is useless. He brings good out of every evil thing in our lives. We don't have to explain to God. We don't have to say, "Now, Lord, You don't understand. You see, So-and-so offended me, and it was very unjust. And because of this, I really cannot—You understand, Lord—I cannot have compassion. Compassion would be unjust." No: Justice is done in compassion. Without compassion, you cannot have justice, because compassion transforms. Compassion frees you. Compassion transforms you into the image of the Father.

And people will look at you and say, "Can you imagine? This man was treated so unjustly, and he forgives." How divine it is to forgive. How divine not to judge. How divine to rejoice, like the father at the prodigal son. How divine to say, "Oh, I'm so glad you're back. I'm so glad you're repentant." Look through the eyes of the Father. Look with the heart of Jesus. Look with the power of the Spirit. The Spirit in you can purify you. The Spirit in you can make you love your brother, though you hate his sin. That is compassionate. Lord, make us all compassionate as the Father is compassionate.

23

Talk to Jesus

You know, a lot of people pray, but they never really talk with God as a Father — as a Dad. "Father" denotes a relationship of love, compassion, joy. A father sees a child running toward him, so excited, and he bounces him up in the air. God bounces you up in the air sometimes; He bounces me too. But He always catches you; He never lets you go. And that's why you and I need to trust that whatever the Father wants is for our good.

This is difficult for us to understand because we feel like we have our whole lives in our hands and we hardly pray to see what God wants. What we do is say, "Lord, would You bless what I want? Would You please do this for me? Now, if You don't do it exactly the way I want it, then there is something wrong with You, Lord. I mean, You must be punishing me because You're not hearing my prayer." God wants to hear us, but He wants to hear something more than "Gimme." He wants to hear something more than, "I want my will! I'm not going to love You." Oh, come on. What would happen if your children said, "I'll love you as long as you always do what I want"?

Don't be a "name-dropper" with God. When we say we want to do something in the Name of Jesus, or we pray in the Name of Jesus, then we have to do it with the attitude of Jesus. We have to know that God, in His infinite mercy, will give us what is best for us. Our Lord used a beautiful example. He said:

> Or what man of you, if his son asks him for bread, will give him a stone? Or if he asks for a fish, will give him a serpent? If you then, who are evil, know how to give good gifts to your children, how much more will your Father who is in heaven give good things to those who ask him! (Matt. 7:9–11)

Why don't you speak up and really talk to God, heart to heart, like a friend? You say a lot of things to friends. Just don't make your prayer one great big supplication, a "want list" that you hand to Him like kids at Christmas. Say, "Hey, Jesus. I love You, Father. I love You with all my heart. And do You know what, Father? I would like this to happen because I think it's for my good. Now, I'm not too sure, but it looks like it's for my good."

Some of us have never spoken to God. I'll bet His ears will really open up when He hears that strange voice coming from below saying, "Help me. Help me. Are You there?" And don't wait until something big and bad happens. Talk to Him about everyday things. Instead of getting all excited about So-and-so, who bugs you to death, say, "Lord, help me with this person who bugs me to death." Jesus had a lot of people who bugged Him.

Remember the parable of the prodigal son — especially the older son who stayed home and did what he was supposed to. It's easy to feel sorry for him. He says, when his father celebrates his brother's return, "I've given you everything. All my life I've obeyed you. I've done everything you've asked me to do. You never once let me celebrate with my friends. And this idiot comes home and you go crazy" (see Luke 15:29–30). Do you feel that little sweet revenge? He didn't mind his brother coming home, but he wanted him taking care of the pigs. He wanted to lord it over him.

That's a purely human, natural way of thinking. But God wants us to rise above that. There's no denial that the younger son did a terrible thing. It's true! But the father said, "Son, all I have is yours. But your brother was dead, and now he's living. What are a ring and a fatted calf? You've got the whole thing" (see 15:31–32). You see how you and I think compared with God? Now, it takes time to think that way, and time is what we call life. Don't worry if you mess up once in a while. Don't worry if you wish somebody would break a leg. (Worry if *you* break his leg.) But when you become aware of that resentful feeling in your heart, say, "Jesus, I don't want to feel this way. I want to be like You." Don't ever minimize the power of prayer.

With great confidence, you must ask the Lord for whatever you're asking for. The Father knows what you need when you pray. Some people say, "If the Father knows what I need, why do I have to ask Him?" He wants you to! One time, the Lord said, "Do not lose heart. Pray without ceasing." That prayer is a compassionate heart, a heart that knows with certainty that God will always answer. Jesus gave us that in the story of that widow who went to the judge and said, "See that justice is done to me." And the judge got so tired, and he said, "This woman's going to pester me to death." And so he gave her what she wanted (see Luke 18:1–8). Jesus is saying, "Ask. Don't ever be afraid. Ask and ask and ask."

But prayer is also about more than asking. The Lord gave us the Our Father, but there are only six words in there that say, "I want something": "Give us today our daily bread." Everything else is praise and glory. You're asking for the Father's will to be done and for grace to forgive. So, you see, that's the secret of prayer: to praise God. You can ask for what you need, but then you ask for God's will to be done.

There's a beautiful combination of praise and love and faith — and then petition. Most people just supplicate. I call them "Gimme prayers." We never talk with God about what *He* wants. It's always what we want. Did you ever think there are other things in the world that are just as important or more important than you are? Have you ever prayed for the world, or your neighbor next door, or your country and your city? Have you ever supplicated God for them with all that vim and vigor and persistence that you supplicate Him for that Cadillac you want? Have you ever gotten to a point where you really trust God?

You know, we worry about a lot of things. The Lord said very definitely that we must trust in His providence. Right after He gave His disciples the Our Father, He said, "Set your hearts on His Kingdom first" (see Matt. 6:33). Pray for the world; pray for your country; pray for your family; pray for your neighbor. Pray for the Kingdom of God to come now, here, and then add your own needs. "But seek first His kingdom and His righteousness, and all these things shall be yours as well. Therefore do not be anxious about tomorrow, for tomorrow will be anxious for itself. Let the day's own trouble be sufficient for the day" (Matt. 6:33–34).

Now, on the one hand, the Lord is talking about trusting in God and not worrying. But He also tells us to be persistent, like the woman and the unjust judge. You might say, "Well, which is it? What am I supposed to do?" Both! You talk to God as a Father. You tell Him everything that's on your heart because speaking to God is prayer. So even if you're talking about your troubles, add to it. Surround it, see? That's what Jesus did with the Our Father. He put the petition in the middle.

If we're truly praying without ceasing, our requests will be surrounded by love, by concern for God and how He's hurt today with all the sins in the world, and how He is offended by nations and countries and cities, and how His glory and His Name are blasphemed everywhere you go. Could you have that in your heart first? Could you have that kind of love for God? Could you say, "Lord, Thy Kingdom come, Thy will be done," and then just in between like a little nut surrounded by chocolate, say, "Jesus, Father, Abba, I need this. I need a job. I need work." And when your first concern is for His righteousness and holiness, for your neighbor, for the Church and the people of God and the nations of the world—then you can pray in His Name. For you will be saying from your heart the prayer of "Jesus, Who is Lord."

24

Giving Freely

We have an if-then mentality: "I will do this for you, but only if you do that for me." There's no sense of giving. And so we lose perspective when it comes to forgiving, to sharing, and to being joyous over other people's good fortune.

Let's look at the parable of the vineyard in Matthew 20. The landowner goes out at daybreak and sees all these workers hanging around. And so he says to them, "You go in my vineyard, and I will give you a fair wage." Well, we know what happened: The landlord got new groups throughout the day, and the last group only worked an hour or so. But when they got paid at the end of the day, every worker all got a denarius—a day's wage. The poor guy who worked all day in the heat of the sun watches as the guy who worked for a cool hour in the evening gets the same wage. "Wait a minute. Have I not worked in the sun? I deserve more." But the landlord replies, "Look, you bargained for a denarius. Are you jealous because I'm generous?" (see Matt. 20:1–16). We must be concerned not with how much we receive but with whether we are giving our very best. We can say this prayer: "Jesus, help me to understand that in order to forgive, I must first give, and give with all my heart; for the measure I shall measure out shall be measured unto me" (see Matt. 7:2).

Remember the servant who was forgiven ten thousand talents, which would be millions and millions of dollars today. The king threatened to throw him in jail and sell his family into slavery but decided to have mercy on him. But then the same servant finds someone who owes him, oh, a few hundred bucks. The man begs for mercy, but the servant throws him in jail until he can pay up (see Matt. 18:23–35). Can you imagine the ingratitude? But God has forgiven our sins—our millions and millions of dollars—and so how can we not forgive our neighbor's little slight? An unforgiving spirit injures the soul.

Jesus said, "Freely I have given to you. Now give freely" (see Matt. 10:8). We must imitate Jesus. There is no one else. We have to find out what Jesus did because the only way to have joy in your heart is to have the virtues of Jesus. And so compassion goes to the point of understanding that my neighbor must work at being holy. We're going to struggle, and we can and should do it together.

God provides so many opportunities to do this, but instead we are ready just to blame. But you'd better look at the beam in your own eye before you go around criticizing everyone else (see Matt. 7:4). You must build. Love builds up our very nature and confidence in our neighbors, whether that neighbor is your family, your friends, or your spouse. We must live up to Jesus' expectations, not our expectations. My neighbor doesn't have to live up to my expectations; he must live up to the expectations of God. If we become preoccupied with our own feeling of perfection, we make ourselves little models, little islands, and everybody else has to measure up. The perfect you is the model for everyone else and you squeeze them into that mold. But everybody is different, and everybody is going to radiate Jesus in a different way. God will do the molding, and He helps you to mold yourself too.

Family life, after all, is teamwork. You've got to work together. You each have your faults, but you all have to build. Children have to build up their families too. And you all have to forgive each other, because divine forgiveness has been given to you time and time again. The measure you measure out, oh boy, is going to be measured out to you. God has willed that each of us should give until there's nothing else to give.

You see, all of creation, all the world, all mankind either benefits or loses out because of you, and so you have got to understand what it means to be loving as Jesus is loving. That means that you love unselfishly. Do you remember Our Lord in the garden? He looked ahead into history and saw all the souls that would not benefit by His death and His Redemption. He saw those who would look at Him and say, "No, I will not forgive this person because he treated me unjustly. I have a right not to forgive." What an awful thing to say to Our Lord. Every time you say the Our Father, you say, "Forgive me in the same way I forgive my neighbor." Just listen to yourself.

Let's examine our consciences. It's hard to do; no one likes it, including me. But go ahead and think of a person whom you don't like, a person you find it very difficult to forgive. Now place yourself before the Almighty God. I want you to look at God and say, "Lord, forgive me for all I have done." And the Lord says, "I will forgive you." "Lord, forgive me for all my infidelity, all my sins, all my mistakes." And He says, "I will forgive you." "Lord, forgive this terrible thing I did." And He says, "I forgive you." Ah, now, here comes your brother. And the Lord of Heaven is looking and saying, "Why, what an opportunity! This person has been forgiven a great debt. I'm going to see what he does." And this neighbor comes to you — someone who has hurt your feelings, embarrassed you in front of a crowd, cheated you, or lied to you. And then you say, "No. I will not forgive."

That means you have a measured love. What you're saying is, "Lord of Heaven and earth, I intend to give this much, and I will not give more." When you do that, you put yourself in a box. You put yourself in a corner and you build a wall around yourself, brick by brick: every resentment, every failure to forgive. You forget that you have been given freely! You don't deserve all the grace that God gives you! He gives it freely! But now, you have to give freely.

So many of us are trapped in our memory, trapped in our understanding, trapped in our will, since we have built these walls. And we start taking them down by forgiving. You can say, "Lord, I want to love as You love, without measure. I want to give freely. I don't want to miss opportunities." Look at everything that comes your way today as an opportunity to radiate the face of Christ in your life. And that is to give. Give of your compassion, your love, your gentleness, your holiness. Give and give freely, and then you will live up to the expectations of Jesus.

25

Christian Identity

I've been thinking about the greatest problem in the world today. I don't mean economic problems or political problems or worldwide problems. I'm talking about problems individuals have in their souls. And I think one of the greatest is identity. People have lost sight of their identity. Now, there's a lot of talk about identity. Everybody wants to know who they are, where they're going, what they're doing. And yet, the reality of another life and the reality of Heaven and God seem to be out of the question. And when you take God out of the question of identity, then you can never find yourself.

People, in an effort to find themselves, *do* everything. Do, do, do, but they never *become*. See, identity is a becoming. It's an understanding of who you are and why you were created by God. We're all running around trying to be somebody else. We look at our neighbor and say, "Oh, it'd be wonderful to have a career, to be a celebrity, to do this, to do that." And we knock ourselves out trying to be what God never asked us or wanted us to be. If a daisy would try to be a chrysanthemum, he would destroy himself. We need daisies just like we need mums.

The people in St. Paul's day had the same problem. In First Corinthians, he talks about the human body made of different parts that each have a purpose. If my hand were to say to an eye, "I want to be the eye," can you imagine your hand popping out of your head? Could you imagine your eye at the end of your arm? It's grotesque. But that's how it is when we keep ourselves in a state of anxiety over our identity, our purpose. We no longer love ourselves when we don't know who we are. We're kind of floating in the air, and you can't love anything if you're just floating.

You must know yourself. You must know your dignity as a child of God. You can do it by knowing God, because God has a special plan for you. And that special plan makes one demand: that you are faithful to the duties of your state in life. If you are a father, be a father. If you are a mother, be a mother. And if you are a child, be a child. When a child decides to be father, and the father decides to be child, and the mother decides to be father, then you have a grotesque body, just as grotesque as if I had an eye in the middle of my hand.

You see, God had a design in store for you and me, and we have to follow that plan. And it's a plan that brings joy in your life. Most of us are unhappy, not because we haven't found our identity but because we're not happy with it. We want to be something else or somebody else. So, if you really want to have joy in your life, you need to know your real dignity as a child of God. Being a child of God *is* your identity; it *is* your dignity. And what you do with that is what we call holiness.

When we lose hope, we lose love. And when we lose love, we fall apart. But see, the Author of Love is in your heart, in the Eucharist, in grace. Every time I look at you, I see Jesus. Try it sometime. Do you know what I like to do? Since the Trinity lives in me, I like to see the Father in me looking at Jesus in you. Do you know what happens when that happens? The Spirit flows between you and me. When the Spirit flows between you and me, we call that love.

God has made the family in the image of the Trinity. All men who are fathers and husbands are made to the image of the Eternal Father. Like the Eternal Father, you are to be compassionate, merciful, provident, and loving. When you die, God is not going to ask you what empire you built or what you accomplished. He's going to look at you and see your compassion and mercy. Think of the father of the prodigal son. He went out every day and looked down the road in hopes of finding his son, who had so wronged him—because he loved him.

You know, most of us are aiming for Purgatory. Aim higher because Jesus wants you to be transformed into His image. And the only way you're going to do that, as a father, is to be like the Eternal Father. So your duty in your family is to provide in the best way you can. Be content with that. Be compassionate and merciful to your wife, to your children, and to yourself. You have to love yourself because God doesn't make junk. He makes beautiful people. And even if you fail, if you have not done what you think you should have done, give that to God. Sometimes fathers take out the regrets and guilt in their own hearts on their children. Don't do that. When you don't know what to do, think of that father in the parable of the prodigal son who kept looking out for his son.

Women are designed by God to be the mortar in the building of the family. The mortar keeps the bricks together. Men are like the brick in a building: They add strength, stability, protection. But without a woman, without that mortar between, it's very difficult. A woman has been designed by God to be gentle, to be humble, to be obedient, to be a bond of reconciliation. Not a doormat! I've always said, "God was good to some man when He gave me a religious vocation." I'd have given him a fit.

What does it mean to be a holy wife? It means that you love your husband and your children, that you're ready to sacrifice for them to bring the love of Jesus to them. And for children, it means that you are ready to obey. I know that sounds lame to lots of kids, but that's where the heroism comes in. The hero is the one who finds joy in obeying.

You know, they have taken away all our heroes. Anybody in the past, even way in the past, who was on any kind of pedestal: We have torn them down totally. The only ones I see on pedestals today are celebrities and rock groups. Believe me, they are not heroes. You are God's heroes. You—husbands and wives and children, the people of God—are His heroes. You are going to help save the world. There is no one else.

You are to be what God made you to be. I see a lot of women come to me and they apologize for being "only" a wife and mother. What else do you want to be? You're living a sacrament. And if you're single? What a beautiful witness of love and joy. If you're divorced and lonely, again, what a fantastic witness to truth and goodness you can be. Don't let the enemy or the world take away from you a treasure. And the treasure is your mission from God, and your mission from God is to be great.

St. Paul said in Second Corinthians, "You are God's incense to the world. You are a letter from Christ" (see 2 Cor. 2:15; 3:3). Just imagine that: God's incense. That is your identity; that is your dignity. If we had a persecution today—one of those juicy ones, the kind where they're looking for you in the streets—could they tell if you were a Christian? Could they tell you're a Christian by the way you act, the way you think, the way you talk? They should be able to. Christianity is much more than a religion: It's a transforming power. And it's a mission!

Now you say, "I'm a career girl," or "I'm a wife," or "I'm this, I'm that." That's secondary. Your mission is to be a *holy* wife, a *holy* career girl, a *holy* technician, a *holy* doctor, a *holy* lawyer, a *holy* ditch digger. You say, "I can't read or write." So? You don't need to read or write if you've got a heart. You can love God.

The wife is the one who finds joy in being a wife. The husband is the one who finds joy in his wife, in his family, and in being faithful. You see, when you're not faithful to God, you're discontent. If you're discontent, you're not going to be faithful, and vice versa. Then that ruins your peace, and when peace is ruined, there is no joy. And that's when you lose your sense of identity. Then you go around looking. Ah, the housewife wants to be a career woman; the husband wants another wife, or a mistress. Children are still wet behind the ears, and they want to be on their own. They don't want to obey.

So we have that grotesque body: We have that eye in the middle of the hand, and that's wrong. And you have to know it's wrong. We need people strong enough to stand tall and say, "This is wrong," and take all the flak that comes from saying that. Have the courage to be what God wants you to be: a holy wife, a holy child, a holy husband. You see, whatever state of life you're in, that's what God has designed for you through the accomplishment of His will in your life. At this moment, wherever you are, that is God's will for you at this moment.

Maybe you don't like it, but that's not the point. It's reality. God either permitted or ordained whatever is happening to you at this moment. What you do with it right now is what's important. This present moment is God's will for you. You can rise above the ashes that you think your life is. Never lose hope. No matter how sinful you are, no matter what a mess your life is, or has been, God can be glorified in you by the very fact that you are a great sinner.

Once you understand that you're His child and that He has a mission for you, that brings joy in your heart. And once you understand that joy, then you're willing to accept your state in life without being dissatisfied, without grumbling about it. You're willing to take the bad and the good, for better or for worse.

Mother M. Angelica
(1923–2016)

Mother Mary Angelica of the Annunciation was born Rita Antoinette Rizzo on April 20, 1923, in Canton, Ohio. After a difficult childhood, a healing of her recurring stomach ailment led the young Rita on a process of discernment that ended in the Poor Clares of Perpetual Adoration in Cleveland.

Thirteen years later, in 1956, Sister Angelica promised the Lord as she awaited spinal surgery that, if He would permit her to walk again, she would build Him a monastery in the South. In Irondale, Alabama, Mother Angelica's vision took form. Her distinctive approach to teaching the Faith led to parish talks, then pamphlets and books, then radio and television opportunities.

By 1980 the Sisters had converted a garage at the monastery into a rudimentary television studio. EWTN was born. Mother Angelica has been a constant presence on television in the United States and around the world for more than forty years. Innumerable conversions to the Catholic Faith have been attributed to her unique gift for presenting the gospel: joyful but resolute, calming but bracing.

Mother Angelica spent the last years of her life cloistered in the second monastery she founded: Our Lady of the Angels in Hanceville, Alabama, where she dedicated herself, alongside her Nuns, to prayer and adoration of Our Lord in the Most Blessed Sacrament.